Building Your Own
Privatized Banking System

Educating Americans on The Purpose of Specially Designed Life Insurance Contracts (SDLIC)

Table of Contents

Acknowledgements

It both saddens and sickens the author of this book to think about our children, grandchildren, and future generations experiencing a lifestyle that is more difficult and challenging than ours because of the lack of economic leadership in America since the 1970's. The trail that we want to blaze for them and the rest of the country is simple: *Educate. Empower. Enlighten.*

We want to thank the Nelson Nash Institute (NNI) for their support of our business model and the game-changing curriculum they provide to financial professionals who strive to educate their clients on solid economic principles. Nelson Nash embarked on his personal journey towards economic freedom by studying Austrian economics and bringing the concept of *infinite banking* into the mainstream so financial services professionals could begin to *think differently* about cash flow, opportunity costs, and the proper *storage* of one's personal wealth. Nelson is a pioneer and a visionary whose life's work will be carried on by NNI through the leadership of David Stearns, Carlos Lara, and Robert Murphy. Thank you gentlemen for your tireless commitment to economic truths. Your *Night of Clarity* events have allowed participants to gleam knowledge from world renowned speakers, like Ron Paul and David Stockman. And your *IBC Think Tank* events provide a place for financial professionals to learn from one another. For anyone seeking more clarity in your personal or business economy, I encourage you to visit www.infinitebanking.org to learn more about this unique organization.

Next, we would like to thank the incredible team of Todd Langford and Kim Butler for their willingness to share their ideas with the financial services community. Todd is the creator of the Truth Concepts™ software. Many properly trained financial professionals who understand the details of structuring privatized banking systems for clients utilize Todd's software as a way to help explain the concept in straight-forward facts and figures. Visit www.truthconcepts.com to learn more about the software's capabilities. Kim Butler is the founder of Partners 4 Prosperity and is a leading author, speaker, and advocate on topics relating to privatized banking strategies. You can find Kim's books on Amazon or her website www.partners4prosperity.com. Kim also writes articles and speaks at various industry events to educate the public on various financial myths.

Garrett Gunderson is the author of two critically acclaimed books, *Killing Sacred Cows and What Would The Rockefeller's Do?* He is also the founder of The Wealth Factory, which is family office that serves entrepreneurs in their efforts to control their economic destiny. If you are an entrepreneur who is looking to get to the *next level* in life, visit www.wealthfactory.com and see if their resources could benefit you. Garrett is a tremendously talented individual whose abundance in sharing his knowledge has allowed the contents of his books to highlight the benefits of *cash flow banking*. After you finish reading this book, we highly recommend you search the internet to grab a copy of each of his masterpieces.

Disclaimer: NNI, Truth Concepts, Partners 4 Prosperity, Wealth Factory, e3 ConsultantsGROUP and Kalos Capital are separate and unrelated companies.

Lastly, we want to thank all of our business colleagues at e3 Wealth, e3 Tax, Ameritime, and SBO Wealth for your invaluable collaboration over the past couple of decades. The financial services industry could learn a lot from our *Unique Ability Teamwork Model* because the days of succeeding as a *rugged individualist* are numbered. Our environment fosters collaboration so that our collective knowledge improves not only the lives of our clients but also all of the stakeholders involved in our business model. It is an honor to work alongside each and every one of you!

ABOUT THE AUTHOR AND THE SOURCE FOR THIS BOOK

John E. Moriarty has been an entrepreneur in the financial services industry since 1995. John is the founder and president of e3 ConsultantsGROUP, a holding company that is made up of four separate and distinct businesses: e3 Wealth, e3 Tax, e3 Marketing, and e3 Real Estate.

John is an investment advisor representative in the State of Missouri and is a designated Chartered Financial Consultant (ChFC). He holds several securities industry exams including the Series 7, 22, 24, 63 and 65 registrations. In addition, John is an Office of Supervisory Jurisdiction (OSJ) Manager, and a licensed life insurance advisor in numerous states.

John believes in *awakening the inner-entrepreneur in all Americans!* This book, along with his first book *Understanding the Secret Language of Money (2014)* are an attempt to provide a path for those people who want to think differently about their money and finance related decisions.

e3 ConsultantsGROUP
10825 Watson Road, Suite 100
Sunset Hills, MO 63127
Office: 314.822.4440 and
Email: jmoriarty@e3wealth.com
www.e3wealth.com

As part of a desire to build a community of entrepreneurial minded financial professionals, e3 Marketing has officially become a part of the Prosperity Economics Movement (PEM). If you are receiving a copy of this book from another financial professional, it is most likely because that individual is part of this crusade or is collaborating with e3 Marketing/PEM to educate the public regarding certain financial concepts.

Once you have finished reading this book, we encourage you to reach out to the financial professional who first introduced the concept of privatized banking to you.

DISCLAIMERS

Financial Planning is challenging. It becomes more challenging as you begin to factor in things such as individual wants and desires. This is compounded by variables such as unique personal circumstances and ever-changing regulations. This book reflects the author's opinions, which are not endorsed by Kalos Capital. These opinions are not intended to provide specific advice and should not be construed as recommendations for any individual. This book is published with the understanding that the author is not engaged in rendering any legal services. Investments involve risk including the potential for loss of the principal amount invested. Past performance is no guarantee of future results. Please remember that investment decisions should be based on an individual's goals, time horizon and tolerance for risk. The services of competent legal, tax and financial professionals should be sought prior to executing any strategy.

Regarding Alternative Investments

Alternative investments are speculative in nature, and may not be suitable for all investors. The strategies employed in the management of such investments involve increased risks, including lack of liquidity and the potential loss of part or the entire principal amount invested.

Regarding Life Insurance Contracts

Any policy guarantees mentioned are based on the claims-paying ability of the issuing life insurance company. The main intent of traditional life insurance contracts is for death benefit protection. Any outstanding loans on a policy will directly reduce the death benefit and decrease the amount of coverage received by the policy's beneficiaries. Interest must be paid back or the death benefit will be further reduced and could actually result in negative cash value. This event could cause the policy to lapse and all policy benefits to be eliminated. Should a policy lapse or be surrendered, any policy gains created internally would cause income taxes for the policy holder.

Ready?

Abundance

Think Differently

Challenge the Status Quo

Take Control of Your Financial Picture

Protect Your Personal/Business Economy

Chapter 1.   PRE-FRAMING OUR DISCUSSION

Before getting into the learning content of this book related to helping you establish an *ideal outcome* when you are finished reading, we need to answer the most common questions of "Why should I listen to this author?" and "Is this book's purpose to just sell me life insurance?". It is vital that you realize what our firm e3 ConsultantsGROUP is all about. **e3 ConsultantsGROUP** is a holding company that operates in four strategic areas of the financial services industry:

e3 Wealth – We oversee $500+ million in assets and provide a family office model to individuals, families, and business owners at all levels of net worth. We have resources available to our clients in almost any area that deals with money: investments, insurance, tax, estate planning, banking, cash flow strategies, Social Security benefit planning, Medicare, and long term care as examples.

e3 Tax – We built our own tax department through strategic acquisitions of several tax practices. e3 Tax serves individuals, families and business owners in the areas of income tax preparation, accounting, bookkeeping, financial reporting, consulting, and cash flow management. Our staff of 20+ highly qualified professionals including several Certified Public Accountants (CPA) and Enrolled Agents. We serve thousands of individual and corporate clients.

e3 Real Estate – e3 combines its resources in the wealth and tax arenas to consult with real estate entrepreneurs in the following areas: cash flow strategies, income tax minimization, financing options, private lending opportunities, strategies regarding the purchase and sale of investment properties (residential and commercial). e3 Real Estate has access to an integrated resource network of financial professionals that assist entrepreneurs with entity creation, asset protection, and overall estate planning.

e3 Marketing – This is our "Research & Development" arm where ideas on better ways to educate the public become a reality. Our Training & Development Program is a critical piece to our business model and provides advisors a cutting-edge learning environment due to the usage of NLP (neuro-linguistic-programming) techniques.

As you can see, we are no ordinary financial firm. We aim to **educate** our clients about strategies that **empower** them to customize their actions and ultimately **enlighten** their future while taking control of their financial picture. In addition to our comprehensive business model, we have hosted weekly radio shows in both St. Louis, MO called "Maximize Your Money" on KFTK 97.1FM (www.971talk.com) and in Austin, TX called "The Advance & Protect Show" at Talk Radio 1370AM (www.talkradio1370am.com).

This is also not our first effort to write a book on a subject that challenges the way you think about money and finance. *Understanding The Secret Language of Money* was written in 2014 to awaken the inner-entrepreneur in all of us. We wrote this book to counter the message from mainstream media and large financial institutions who believe there is very little value in owning cash value life insurance for the majority of Americans. If you spend any time listening to people like Dave Ramsey or Suzie Orman, you know their opinion of cash value life insurance. Some of the *talking heads* will tell you that cash value life insurance is *too expensive*, *a horrible investment*, or a product insurance agents sell only because they are paid a large commission to do so!

Luckily for you, the reader, our perspective on this topic is based on tens of thousands of knee-to-knee appointments with individuals, families, and business owners. We will not give you our *opinion* on this topic blindly with no consideration for your actual financial situation. Instead, we will provide both concepts and strategies that demystify cash value life insurance as a financial vehicle that has tremendous potential to provide you flexibility, access, and control of your money. If **designed properly** and **monitored frequently** by a financial professional who is **properly trained** in cash flow strategies and alternative asset classes, your opinion of cash value life insurance may change significantly.

The purpose for writing this book is to help you achieve a better understanding of certain key topics that can substantially improve your personal or business economy. We believe everyone who has positive cash flow and good habits with money deserves to hear about how a specially designed life insurance contract (SDLIC) can be utilized as both an alternative asset class and a cash flow tool. If you believe in minimizing your risk in your portfolio and want to pay cash for big ticket items in your personal and/or business economy, then we urge you to keep reading.

Keeping more of what you make and earning more on your money is the mindset our firm as well as helping our clients reduce the impact of market volatility, inflation, taxes and longevity in their financial pictures. We believe it is critical for financial professionals to change the way they communicate with their clients and prospects about money and financial related decisions. Why now? Because our economy is not functioning on solid fundamentals! We believe people need to *think differently* if you want to take control of your financial picture. Conservative savers are being forced to deal with a financial future that involves *more risk, not less!*

While accumulation strategies are definitely important in a saver's personal or business economy, proper utilization strategies allow people to control the flow of their money while it works for them. We call this phenomenon **uninterrupted compound growth.** To understand this concept, you also need to realize that there are three different *types of return* you can create with your money.

Chapter 2.   TYPES OF RETURN

Habits are the key to financial success. It doesn't matter how much money you make, save, inherit, or receive if you don't have the simple habits of *saving first and spending less money than you have available*. Otherwise, your financial picture could be in jeopardy. For many of you, it would be prudent to make your assets work for you by putting your money into asset classes that create growth through income first. This chapter is designed to help you realize that you have several ways to create returns.

Internal return is what your asset generates through its performance (both income and appreciation over time). In most cases, this is calculated as the return on investment (ROI). Most retail, market-driven vehicles (stocks, mutual funds, and exchange-traded funds [ETFs]) use this return to measure their performance. They provide reports that show average returns over a specific period (one year, five years, ten years, and since inception). Your internal return is specific to your timeline of action and cannot be truly determined until after you've completed your investment horizon.

And always remember that *past performance is no indication of future results*. You hear this all the time, but some financial advisors may disregard this principle when making investment recommendations. But **internal return is normally out of your control** because you have no way to know how much appreciation you'll earn from the market. Utilizing asset classes that generate growth through income first can assist you in creating a more stable internal return.

External return is rarely considered, but entrepreneurs and institutions take advantage of this economic benefit all of the time. Think of it as your *return on cash flow*. When you properly utilize your money and leverage your internal return by getting more of your money to flow into your control, the results are magnified. You can do this by minimizing the opportunity costs that impact your daily life, such as:

- Interest costs from banks, credit cards, and mortgage companies
- Lack of control of your principal as you pay down debt
- Restricting the use of your money to one goal only
- Being held hostage by income taxes when you want to access your money

External return is *subjective* because everyone's financial picture is different. When an entrepreneur buys a business, its initial internal return is based on annual growth and business valuation. Now the buyer can add an external return by reducing expenses through operational synergies, improved employee morale with a better work environment, and visionary leadership. Add in some management expertise that can improve the trajectory of the company's future, and all of a sudden the value of the business could improve.

You can accomplish something similar by operating your personal economy the same way. You first need to realize that *cash flow is everything*. Managing your budget to keep spending on a realistic path while simultaneously building savings is extremely difficult. But if you can follow sound financial principles within your own financial home, generations of your family can enjoy the benefits.

Next, you should implement financial strategies that get money flowing into your control without completely depleting your savings or access to capital. Paying off credit card debt, student loans, and your home is a very beneficial financial strategy, but if you leave yourself with zero savings to accomplish these goals, you could wind up vulnerable should an unexpected event occur with your job, health, or family that affects you financially. So figuring out ways to have your money work for you while you use it is critical, and we'll discuss those techniques later in this book.

Let's look at a few examples just to get a sense of this concept:

Example 1: Paying Off Debt

Let's say you have fifty thousand dollars ($50,000) of household income and twenty thousand dollars ($20,000) in the bank making virtually nothing (less than 1 percent interest). Your monthly debt payments are:

- A $500 payment to low-interest credit cards with a $10,000 balance at 5 percent interest
- A $250 student loan payment with a $10,000 balance at 5 percent interest

This $750 per month adds up to nine thousand dollars ($9,000) per year or 18 percent of your income.

Should you pay off these debts with the $20,000 of cash you have in the bank? Conventional wisdom says that doing so will save you the 5 percent interest paid to the credit card and student loan companies (this is the internal rate of return).

But what is your increased cash flow when you pay off the debts? It's the amount you no longer pay out per year: $9,000 or 18 percent. This is the sum of the 5 percent internal rate of return plus the 13 percent external return from the principal.

However, this comes with an opportunity cost: the lack of cash for an emergency fund. In other words, liquidity is eliminated while cash flow is dramatically increased.

Another option is to pay off the credit card first and then pay off the student loan in the next year or so. You pay off the credit card first because it has a higher return on cash flow for the same amount of debt ($500 per month saved is a 12-percent increase to cash flow).

Example 2: Paying Off Your Home

In this example, you have $100,000 in household income. You have a $150,000, thirty-year mortgage at 4 percent. Your required house payment is only $716 in principal and interest (we'll leave out taxes and insurance because some people build these costs into their payment, and others pay them separately). You are also very conservative and don't like debt of any kind, so you also pay $284 extra to reduce your principal faster totaling $1,000 each month.

You have $200,000 sitting in the bank, making less than 1 percent interest. What happens if you pay off your mortgage now with $150,000 from your savings? You'd save twelve thousand dollars ($12,000) per year in cash flow, an increase of 12 percent (8 percent external return plus 4 percent internal).

What are your opportunity costs? You have less liquidity—you cannot access your $150,000 anymore when you put it into the house unless you sell the property or take out another mortgage (or home equity loan). In other words, the money "in" the home stops working for you—it's making a 0-percent internal return.

Many clients ask, "Doesn't the house still appreciate?" Well, we hope so. But if it does, it appreciates whether you have a mortgage on the property or not. So, no, the $150,000 mortgage payoff in this case *is not working for you*. This is one big reason I am a proponent of certain types of alternative assets for these types of big-ticket items. If structured properly, certain assets can produce both internal and external returns *while* you use the money.

Now I am sure some readers are wondering, *which return is more valuable to me—internal or external?* That's not the way to look at them, though. Instead, you need to look at your financial picture and see how each return impacts your personal economy. The lower your asset values, the greater impact external returns will have on your financial picture.

Example 3

You make $100,000 and have $100,000 in assets. If you save 10 percent of your income ($10,000 per year), that is an external return that *you control*. To create the same accumulation results compared to your cash flow, you would need to make a 10-percent internal return on your assets. Based on our current economy, how much risk are you willing to take to achieve that 10 percent—knowing that you could also lose money?

Now realize, if you have accumulated more assets, the effectiveness of your internal return is magnified.

Example 4

You make $100,000 and have $500,000 in assets. You save the same amount as above (a 10-percent external return on your income). But now you only need to generate a 2-percent internal return to equal your cash flow results. However, the more assets you accumulate, the bigger the risk of loss.

You still want to save 10 percent of your cash flow, but you also want your assets working for you as hard as possible without too much risk. You must find an investment strategy that minimizes risk while achieving an expected internal return. Your financial professional needs to align with it.

Let's compare strategies for accumulating $500,000.

- Saving ten thousand dollars ($10,000) per year and earning a 0-percent internal return, it would take you fifty years.
- With a 5-percent internal return, you cut that time almost in half (25.7 years).
- With an 8-percent internal return, it takes twenty-one years.
- With a 10-percent internal return, it takes nineteen years.

All of these calculations assume that you earn these internal rates every year without interruption—that's not very realistic. The more internal return you seek to create, the more important a risk minimization strategy becomes.

Most people who are successful at building first-generation wealth intend to leave legacies for multiple generations to use and carry forward. This is what I call one's **Eternal return**. It is the culmination of your time, talent, and capital passed on to the next generation. It can be comprised of assets, the knowledge you impart to your family during your life, and the goodwill you have created for your family legacy, etc. This type of return includes a lot of intangibles and is sometimes difficult to grasp but make no mistake—it could be the most valuable return of all. If structured properly, the wealth you've created can improve your family's personal economy five, ten, twenty, even a hundred times over because its members are now working from a more robust, solid foundation that *you* built over time. Our organization believes in teaching our clients *generational planning exercises* that can assist people in optimizing their eternal return.

With an uncertain economic outlook for America over the next thirty years, families that provide an eternal return to their next generations may be protecting not only their personal economies but their families' economic survival. We have a real sense of urgency to teach this information to you because we believe economic forces are working against savers.

The charts on page 16 illustrate as borrowers were benefitting from a 30+ year decline in interest rates, savers were being punished as interest paid on balances in their bank accounts shrank.

Source: Board of Governors of the Federal Reserve System (US)
Shaded areas indicate US recessions - 2014 research.stlouisfed.org

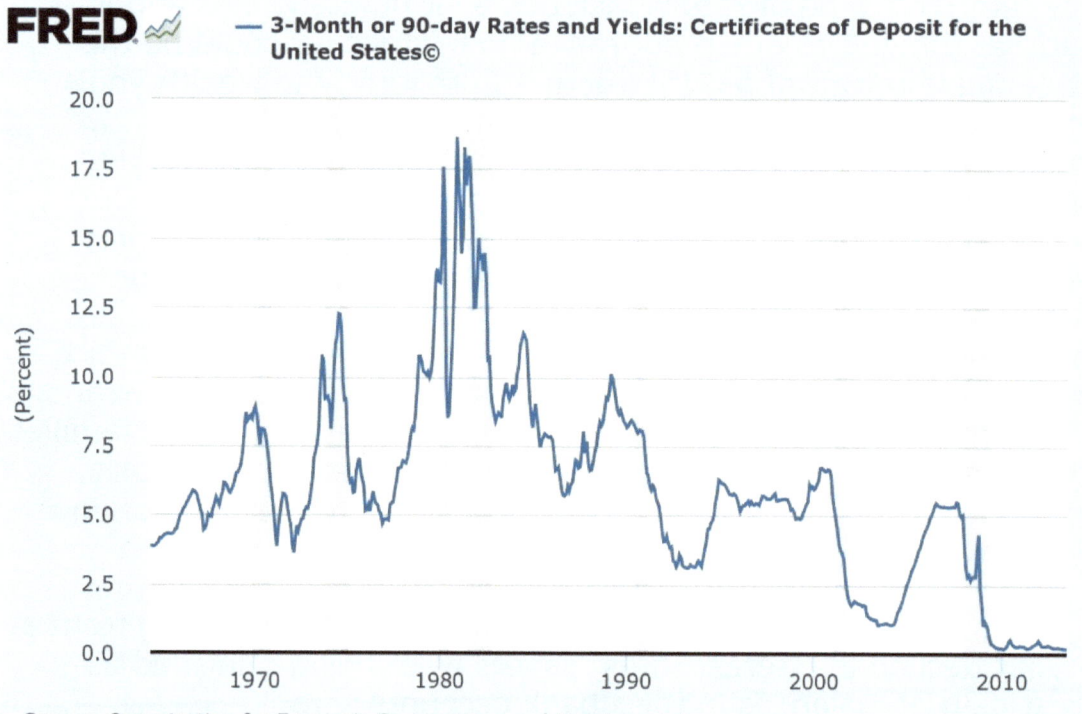

Source: Organisation for Economic Co-operation and Development
Shaded areas indicate US recessions - 2014 research.stlouisfed.org

And, while interest rates were going down, the outstanding debt for our country and the Federal Reserve's balance sheet increased significantly! Over this period of time, Americans were encourage to keep consuming and take risk with their money to keep the economy alive and promote equity investments as opposed to keeping money "on the sidelines" in cash and continue saving.

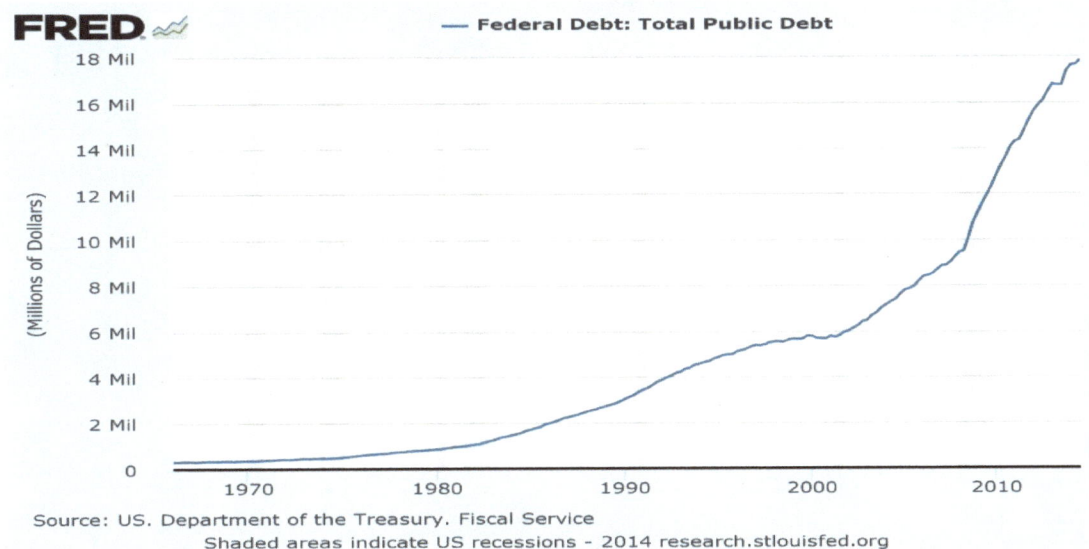

Source: US. Department of the Treasury. Fiscal Service
Shaded areas indicate US recessions - 2014 research.stlouisfed.org

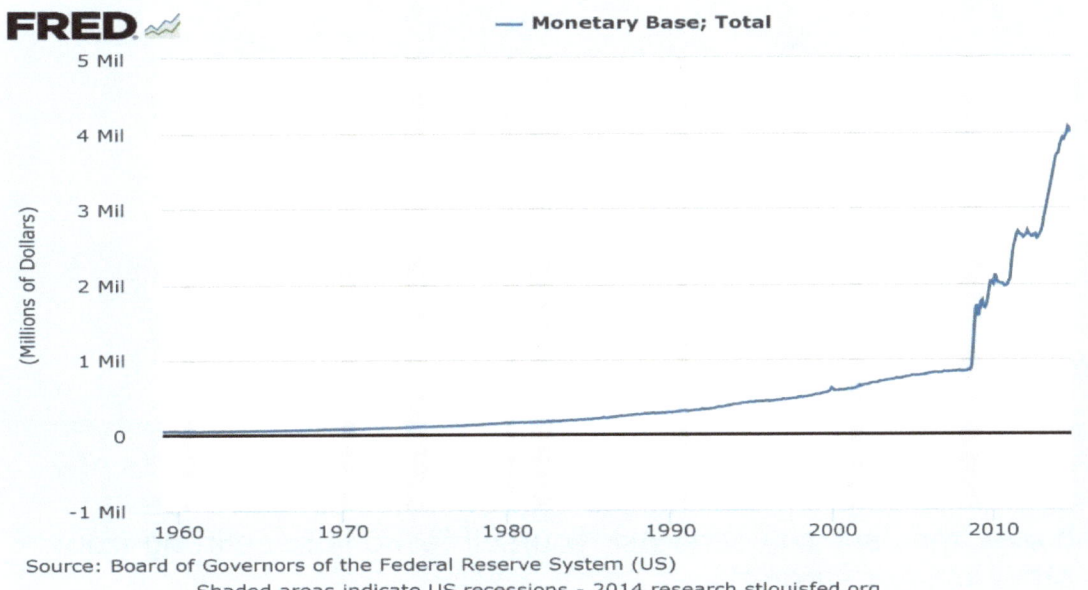

Source: Board of Governors of the Federal Reserve System (US)
Shaded areas indicate US recessions - 2014 research.stlouisfed.org

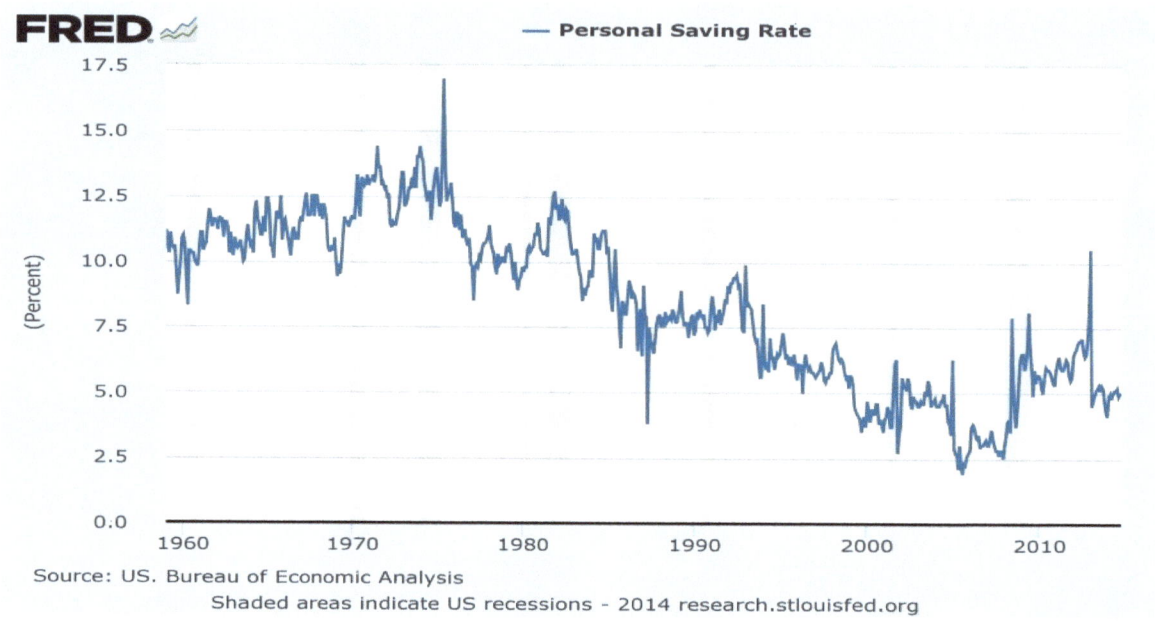

Source: US. Bureau of Economic Analysis

Shaded areas indicate US recessions - 2014 research.stlouisfed.org

Source: S&P Dow Jones Indices LLC

Shaded areas indicate US recessions - 2015 research.stlouisfed.org

These charts above show that since the 1960's, people's habits of saving money deteriorated but the stock market has continued to climb over the past 10 years. Ask yourself "Who is benefitting from this stock market surge?"

What does all of this mean for the conservative saver? In today's economy, cash is earning very low interest and yet trillions of dollars are sitting in banks. We believe bonds can no longer function the same way in a traditional portfolio. And stocks appear to be the remaining traditional option with long term growth potential but the market is much more volatile and the economy seems rather unstable.

Meanwhile, a saver's personal economy is getting more risk averse. Their good money habits are working against them due to market intervention by the U.S. Government, the Federal Reserve, and financial institutions. A saver that wants to utilize their money right now in the present is afraid of how those actions might negatively impact their future! Savers need guidance and alternative strategies right now that provide solutions for both the short term and long term horizon simultaneously.

Chapter 3.   Our Definition of Banking

Our firm believes there are different elements to *banking* and we believe how each element functions in your personal/business economy is critical for people to understand. Actually, you could define *banking* in different ways:

- Paying your bills out of your checking account on a month-to-month basis (Managing your finances)
- Financing purchases with money you don't currently have in your possession (Borrow money)
- Paying cash for a purchase out of your savings/money market account (Save money)

No matter what method or methods of banking you operate under, everyone has two areas of focus with their money:

1) Making money and earning a living in his or her occupation, career, or business so you can begin to save, invest, and utilize your hard earned dollars.

2) Managing your personal or business economy through strategic financing and cash flow awareness with your money-to-month expenses and big ticket purchases.

For several years, our firm has been doing research to determine why today's traditional banking system doesn't appear to benefit savers as it used to over the past 30+ years. Since banks have long been a place for people to **store money**, the reasons behind this action were simple – banks provided **SAFETY** of principal, **LIQUIDITY** through access to your money at any time, and **GROWTH** through interest on any account balance you **kept at the bank**.

Today's relationship between banks and savers has changed dramatically. Now savers are earning less than 1% on their bank accounts because banks don't need any more deposits to function. Subsequently, the Federal Reserve is punishing savers and increasing the risks associated with inflation, taxes and longevity in a saver's economy. Just look at these ads from two different banks to get some perspective:

The first advertisement is from a bank with an offer to pay 5.1% interest on a business sweep account back in 2007. The second advertisement shows an offer from another bank for a "high yield" 12-month CD in 2014. It will pay 1% interest to function in a similar way the sweep account did back in 2007 – but pay 80% less in interest. What's wrong with this picture? Do savers deserve to earn 80% less on their hard earned savings at a time when they desire **more** safety, liquidity, and growth? Or, is it time to look for a different financial institution to assist you with the purpose of your safe money?

Cash Flow Awareness

One of the main things our firm has learned from studying behavioral finance (mentioned later in this book) is that most people with *good money habits* make financial decisions in certain ways. To understand this *decision-making paradigm*, you first need to understand what certain words mean to people with good money habits. Here are the subjective definitions we have given certain words based on tens of thousands of conversations with clients on the topics of money and finance.

Saving: To accumulate money in places where there is little to no risk of one's principal. By saving, the person is not concerned about the return ON their money but rather the focus is on the return OF their money. Saving is normally a conscious act by someone with good money habits and for decades it has resulted in people building up balances in various bank accounts (checking, savings, money market, and certificate of deposits).

Investing: To put money to work in specific assets or financial vehicles that have the *potential* to generate a return on the principal. Your principal becomes your *initial investment* and you become an *investor.* If successful, you will receive a **return on investment (ROI)** or what we called in the last chapter an **internal return**. Note: the process of investing involves the risk of losing your principal and there are many different types of risk that investors face. Determining the appropriate amount of risk for each investment is a subjective process and needs to be measured based on an individual's personal/business economy.

Spending: When someone *plans to spend their money* in the context of good money habits, it means they are paying for either normal variable monthly expenses to **maintain their lifestyle** or they are purchasing big ticket items to **improve their lifestyle.** Note: these items are not the normal, reoccurring expenses that people associate with the act of *paying their bills*.

Here are some examples of different types of *planned spending*:

Maintaining Your Lifestyle: Pay your income taxes, cover unforeseen emergencies, assist a family member, household upkeep, healthcare, etc.

Improve Your Lifestyle: Home improvements, new autos, travel, children's education, gifts, additional real estate, buying a business, etc.

When a person with good money habits *spends* their money, that principal is viewed as being *gone forever*. There is an **opportunity cost** present when this happens as their principal is no longer able to generate any type of return in the future. We call this an **external return** because the money is no longer in your control. Our intention is to help someone choose to spend their money while reducing or eliminating certain opportunity costs over their lifetime. It's important to understand the dynamic between these three words – SAVE, INVEST, and SPEND – and why some people confuse their meaning.

For example, it is possible for someone to invest or spend money without actually saving it first. We would not consider this person to be a conservative saver because they are most likely taking on *more risk* with their investments and could be spending through the *use of debt.* Not all types of debt are bad but debt does add more risk...

On the other hand, there are many people who are not comfortable with the idea of risk and choose to save but never truly invest. This type of saver usually accumulates money in their bank accounts, works hard to pay off their debts as soon as possible, and struggle with the idea of spending their *hard earned money.* This occurs because they possess a fear about the unknown future and this person is constantly worried about *needing their money in case of an emergency.*

We want to help our clients realize their good money habits of *saving first* actually provide them with more flexibility, access, and control of their money. Whether they invest or spend those dollars is up to them; after all, **it's your money!** Here's how we help our clients visualize the process of taking control of their personal/business economies:

Cash Flow Awareness Model

ADVANCE & PROTECT

GOOD MONEY HABITS

SAVE $$$ (Where Do You *STORE* Your Savings?)

< Utilization Strategies >

INVEST (Risk) → Internal Return

SPEND (Opportunity Cost) → External Return

As the diagram above illustrates, the *act of saving* occurs prior to the decision to *invest or spend* for someone with good money habits. We call this process **Cash Flow Awareness.** Whether someone saves money on a monthly basis or accumulates money in big chunks due to financial windfalls (i.e. bonus, commissions earned, business distribution, inheritance, etc.), they are going to **store that money** some place safe until allocating it between investments or current spending needs & wants. The process of storing money in a safe place is called **accumulation** and the process of deciding whether to invest or spend your savings is called **utilization.**

Utilization strategies are seldom a topic financial professionals educate their clients about when discussing their financial pictures. Our industry is usually zeroed in on investment conversations and the majority of financial vehicles that exist in the marketplace today revolve around a risk/return mindset. The thinking is that in order to achieve higher returns, an investor must be prepared to take on more risk in their financial picture. Our focus with utilization strategies centers around four main questions concerning a client's cash flow awareness:

- What is the purpose of your money? To Invest or Spend?

- What is the time horizon for each purpose? Long Term or Short Term?

- Are their specific risks you would like to minimize over that time frame?

- Where do you currently store your savings?

Getting answers to these questions allows the financial professional to act as an *advocate* for their clients' best interests. Ultimately, we aim to teach our clients to simply **discover** what dollars are flowing into your control and what dollars are flowing out of your control. Then, **strategize** so more money flows into your control. The **end result** will be more money for you to retain and utilize during your lifetime and more money for future generations.

Chapter 4.   Building a Successful Business

Over the past several years, our firm has assisted hundreds of entrepreneurial business owners with the task of *financing* the growth of their business. Because of our experiences in dealing with business owners when they are implementing various decisions related to money, we thought it would make sense to *dive deeper* into this process for the readers of this book. Any competent saver in today's economy will be faced with similar scenarios, especially if you run your household finances *like a small business*.

In order to start a business, the first thing you need is **CAPITAL**. What are the main sources of capital for business owners?

Borrowing from a Bank

Getting money from a bank is the normal method of raising capital for a business, assuming you qualify for a loan. Once the loan is approved, the bank will structure the terms of the loan for you. The bank structures an immediate repayment plan for you while controlling the amount of principal and interest paid back through the amortization schedule. That monthly payment is an expense most businesses prioritize, so that you don't default on the loan.

Building up Personal Assets

For some business owners, it's difficult to get a loan from a bank. Sometimes it's because your credit isn't strong enough to qualify and other times your business type is just at the idea stage or service driven and until you are able to show a profit, no capital is available. In these instances, many of our clients would focus on saving money first in order to invest in opportunities with greater return on investment (ROI) potential. Why would someone take this type of risk with his or her hard earned savings? Well, when you have good habits with saving money in the bank but realize your money could be working harder (or smarter) for you, controlling your future by opening a business appears to be a good alternative.

Your Top Priority is Cash Flow

Once the *door is opened* to your business, the number one priority is to create strong cash flow as soon as possible. Positive cash flow will result from a good **awareness** between what expenses **need** to be paid on a month-to-month basis and those big ticket purchases that are the **wants** in your business plan. Those wants come at different levels. They may start out as purchasing items for day-to-day operations (buying furniture, small equipment, vehicles, advertising, etc.) and over time, the size of the wants expand as your business is growing (buy a new building, invest in larger equipment, acquire another competitor, etc.). The important thing to understand in this situation is that you **STORE** your cash flow in a place where it's safe, liquid, and achieving some level of growth.

Creating Strong Cash Flow

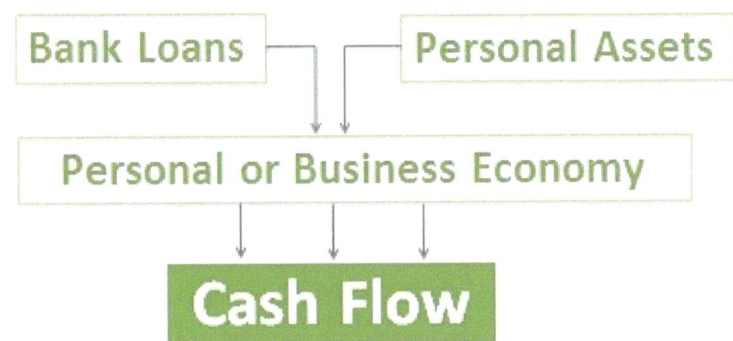

A successful company operates in a manner where surplus cash flow quickly provides them **OPTIONS** as to where cash flow is allocated in the future. These decisions are usually made in a strategic manner and our firm recommends you communicate with your tax and wealth professionals to discuss all possible scenarios. We've summarized three of the most common scenarios our business clients implement with their cash flow:

#1 Accelerate the Repayment of Bank Loans

Most business owners strive to have the least amount of debt possible. The thought is the faster a financial institution is repaid, the more control an owner will have in their business economy. So, accelerating the repayment of a loan is a frequent use of excess cash flow and capital. Once the loan is paid in full, the owner's financial stability is dramatically improved.

#2 Build Up Personal Assets

If a business' financial health appears to be in good shape, the owner may determine that distributing excess cash flow to one's personal accounts would be advisable. This action could create peace of mind for the owner and his/her family. Dollars could accumulate as savings for future big ticket purchases such as automobiles, children's education, home improvement, or travel. At the same time, these savings could also support longer-term goals such as meeting retirement objectives, healthcare uncertainties, or additional business opportunities.

#3 Build Up Business Assets

When a business is successful, one of the best usages of excess cash flow is to reinvest those funds back **INTO THE BUSINESS**! Creating resources for big ticket purchases or investments can increase your internal rate of return through revenue growth, operational efficiencies, or boost bottom line profits. There are multiple ways to expand one's business: hiring new employees, purchasing strategic equipment, or possibly buy a new building to add much needed space. Other items that can cause your cash flow to increase and improve your return on investment (ROI) would include upgrades to your technology, advertising and marketing.

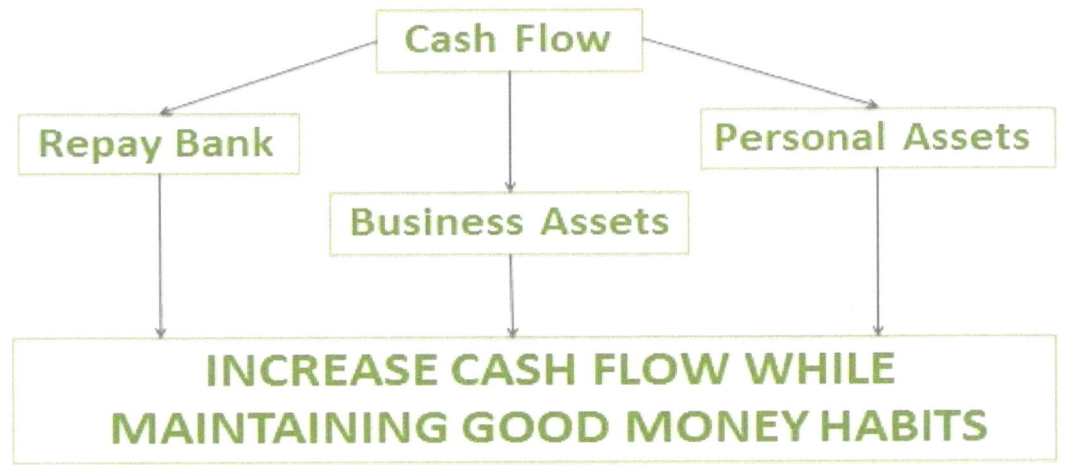

Opportunity Costs

While improving the ROI of a business is a top priority for an owner, it's also important to minimize any opportunity costs that materialize from certain decisions. Most people don't understand the concept of opportunity costs but essentially they can be described as something you give up or pay when you make a decision. When you use excess cash flow to repay a bank loan, the bank ends up controlling more of your principal. Re-investing money into personal assets means those assets are flowing into traditional asset classes and become susceptible to different risks, fees, and potential illiquidity. Even when you pay cash for big ticket purchases in a business, you face opportunity costs. This happens because that cash is now gone and it is no longer working for you earning interest.

The other thing you need to realize is that before you put your money to work for you, those dollars will *sit* somewhere. Another way to look at this situation is to consider your savings as being *stored* somewhere at all times and ask yourself *"Is this storage facility providing me or my business any added value?"*

As you repay the bank, your payments go towards both interest (the bank's profit) and principal (replenishing the bank's loan capabilities).

29

When dollars are re-allocated from your business to your personal accounts, that money is invested into different financial institutions (banks, brokerage firms, mutual funds, etc.) with a focus on **accumulation**, not utilization. And if you keep money in your business today, you're normally storing those dollars in some sort of bank account earning very low interest (less than one percent). These types of scenarios have individuals, families, and entrepreneurs very concerned because they continue to struggle to find a place to store their money. They want flexibility, access, and control of the flow of their money but traditional financial institutions are not providing adequate solutions. So, how does someone establish an alternative *safe money solution* for their personal and/or business economy instead of leaving money in their bank?

Our firm believes today's conservative saver with good money habits needs to consider utilizing a different financial institution to **store** their money while they are waiting to **use it**. In essence, you can create your own **Privatized Banking System** through **Specially Designed Life Insurance Contracts (SDLIC)**.

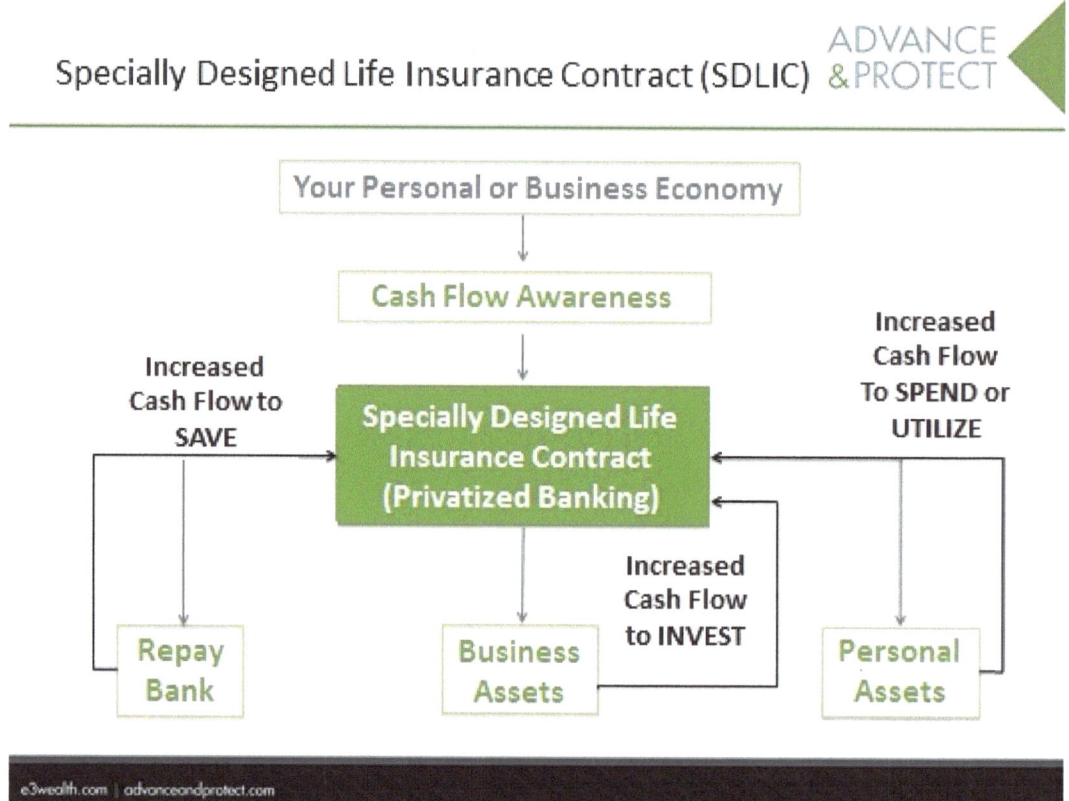

Chapter 5.   WHY PRIVATIZED BANKING AND SDLIC?

Through extensive research and a broad knowledge base on different financial institutions, we believe there are specific types of life insurance companies that offer specific types of life insurance contracts with certain beneficial features to a conservative saver. A properly trained financial professional can use these contracts to offer a conservative saver a tremendous alternative to traditional banking methods. *Please understand that we are not actually creating a real bank for our clients or communicating that life insurance companies are the same as a bank.* Rather we are attempting to design a financial vehicle that can mimic certain **banking functions** in one's personal/business economy – like financing big ticket purchases and controlling where your cash flow is stored.

Not all life insurance companies or products fit the SDLIC model. Certain components must be present for a SDLIC to be optimized:

- Become insured by a Mutual Insurance Company with strong financials
- Use a participating whole life contract with design flexibility
- The contract must allow for access to the policy cash value through policy loans while the policy is being capitalized (the first 5-7 years of the policy)
- Use a contract that allows for policy loans that do not interrupt the compounding of the guaranteed interest and dividends within the policy (These are called a **direct and non-direct recognition loans**)

Very few life insurance companies have all of these components. Later in this book, we will provide you with more supporting data on just how specialized this type of policy design has become. It is important to work with a firm who truly understands and continues to educate themselves on the nuances of this strategy. Several of our advisors have received advanced education on this strategy through the Nelson Nash Institute (NNI). To learn more about this organization, you can visit their website www.infinitebanking.org.

Mutual Insurance Companies

A mutual insurance company (MIC) is an insurance company owned entirely by its policyholders. Any profits earned by a MIC are returned to the policyholders in the form of dividend distributions.[1] The concept of a MIC in the United States dates back to the mid-1700s as a way to pool risks associated with an unexpected loss. Life insurance companies that resemble a mutual structure number less than 50 in the U.S. today. This is due to the conservative nature of MICs. As financial institutions (banks, brokerage firms, and insurance companies) began to change their focus in the 1970's and 1980's towards bottom line profits and became more aggressive in their risk-taking strategies, MIC's resisted market fads and focused on proven techniques designed to build their capital and increase their financial stability.

Our company's research has determined there are a select few of the top rated ("A" or above) insurance companies maintaining a mutual structure. Their financial strength is a core reason we communicate SDLIC policies as a safe money alternative to putting cash in the bank or allocating money to bonds. FDIC protection for banks is a huge conversation point with the public, so it is important to note that all insurance companies pay into a state regulated fund in every state they do business in. This fund's purpose is similar to FDIC for banks – to provide a safety net for policyholders should an insurance company go out of business. This is one of the main reasons whole life insurance contracts issued by MIC's are the "contract of choice" for SDLIC.

Components of a SDLIC

Building a specially designed life insurance contract is all about optimizing the different components of a whole life insurance policy. Here are the main components that can be customized:

Guaranteed Cash Value: This is the amount of cash value available in the policy that is contractually guaranteed. Dividends are added to the guaranteed cash value to get the total cash value in a policy.

Dividends: A dividend paid to your policy represents your share of the mutual insurance company's divisible surplus. The dividend is paid on the anniversary date of your policy. For tax purposes, a policy dividend is treated as a return of capital by the IRS and is not taxable to the policy owner.
You may elect to receive dividends in any of the following options:

---

[1] Investopedia, "Mutual Insurance Company," http://www.investopedia.com/terms/m/mutualcompany.asp

- Paid in Cash (note: if your dividends received exceed your premiums paid at some point, you will create a taxable event)
- Apply to your Premium Payment (lowering future premiums)
- Accumulate Dividends at Interest (interest earned will create a taxable event)
- Use Dividends to Purchase Paid Up Additions (this is the option always recommended with SDLIC)

Once dividends are paid into a policy they are added to the guaranteed cash value and receive compound interest. At this point the dividend is treated as part of the policy cash value for the insured's entire life.

Paid Up Additions (PUA): Paid Up Additions can be added to a whole life contract as a rider or purchased with policy dividends. PUA's immediately increase the cash value in a policy and also become part of the death benefit. PUA's are treated as a *single premium insurance contract* added to your base policy and allow more design flexibility with SDLIC. PUA's receive their own dividends and those dividends receive compound interest when they remain in the policy.

PUA's can be *level or a one-time single premium* (LPUA or SPUA). SPUA's are received in the first year of the policy and normally result from another policy's cash value being transferred into a SDLIC. This transfer is called a 1035 Exchange. This type of transfer protects the cash value from the old policy from being taxed and it also protects the new SDLIC from becoming a Modified Endowment Contract (MEC). We will discuss MEC's in a little bit.

Term Rider: Depending on the design of a SDLIC, the age of the insured and the health of the insured, additional term insurance may need to be added to the policy in the early years in order to avoid the SDLIC becoming a MEC. This term rider is normally removed after 10 years to optimize the cash value accumulation of the SDLIC.

Now that you are aware of the components in a SDLIC, it's time to explain how a competent financial professional will properly build a SDLIC and customize it to fit your personal or business economy. The three main components to build a SDLIC are the **Base Premium, Level Paid Up Additions (LPUA),** and the **Term Rider**. A properly structured SDLIC needs to have adequate early cash values for the policy owner to access while also building a solid dividend scale that creates long term cash value accumulation in the policy. This feat is accomplished by balancing the amount of your annual premiums that are split between Base and LPUA. The trick is to properly allocate enough premiums to both in order to optimize the long term performance of a SDLIC. Too much base premium may build a strong dividend scale but sacrifice short term access to cash values because there won't be any! A larger amount of LPUA's will get you more early cash value but may impact your long term growth of dividends and have your policy susceptible to interest rate fluctuations. Most traditional whole life policies are built with 100% of the premiums going towards the base premium. This helps develop a strong, long-term dividend scale but causes the cash value growth in the policy to grow very slowly. This is why most people think a permanent, whole life policy is a *horrible investment* because they don't have any cash value build up for five, seven, sometimes 10 years.

With SDLIC, a policy will be designed where the base premium is 30%-50% of the total premium and PUA's are 50%-70% of the total premium. This design should optimize long-term dividends, increase early cash value access and increase flexibility in utilizing your policy. It is important to understand that this type of policy design does have some limitations. There are certain tests the insurance company must perform on a SDLIC to make sure it is not a Modified Endowment Contract (MEC). If a policy becomes a MEC, it will lose the tax preferential treatment of loans and operate more like an annuity. To protect against a MEC design, there needs to be a certain amount of policy death benefit in the early years of the contract (7-10 years) to meet the MEC guidelines. Working with a financial professional that understands both the specific policy and income tax limitations on a SDLIC is paramount to this process.

When is SDLIC not a good fit?

A financial strategy such as implementing a SDLIC is not appropriate in all financial pictures. It is important to understand what type of situation should give someone pause before moving forward with SDLIC.

If someone or a family is not good at saving, this strategy is not a good fit. Good habits with money are a must for SDLIC to be effective. Without them, this strategy would fail before it starts due to the temporary illiquidity in the design. Any person setting up a SDLIC needs to understand that they will not have access to 100% of their money for 5 to 7 years, depending on the age and health of the insured and the capitalization by the owner. In essence, the lack of liquidity is covering the cost of the permanent life insurance you are establishing with your SDLIC. To disregard the lack of 100% liquidity would be careless. However, it is also important to remember how one can put the money to work that's inside of a SDLIC immediately. Utilizing the available cash value while you wait for all of your money to be accessible is a strategic way to minimize the impact of the temporary illiquidity. But if someone needs access to all of their money immediately (from day one), this strategy may not be a good fit. That is why it is so important for a client to work with a seasoned financial professional who looks at your entire financial picture before making any recommendation.

Understanding the tax rules is critical as well with a SDLIC. Avoiding an accidental or purposeful MEC design, proper withdrawals/policy loans and effective capitalization needs to be done while receiving competent income tax advice. Consider that if the policy is surrendered or it lapses while the insured is still alive, there could be negative income tax consequences. Please make sure the financial professional(s) you are working with understand the section of the IRS Tax Code that pertains to permanent life insurance (IRC Section 7702).

Proper capitalization of a SDLIC can minimize a lot of potential problems being mentioned. If you do not fund the contracts in a manner where they maximize the base and LPUA rider within the first 3-5 years, it is possible that policy could underperform causing your cash value growth to be less than expected. Underperformance would then be magnified as the contract experiences loan activity. If you are planning to utilize the policy early in its setup (within the first 24 months), it is imperative that you continue to capitalize the policy through year five or at least begin a payback of the policy loan in some minor capacity. The compounding impact of the interest accumulating in a policy that has early loan activity without proper capitalization or loan payback could very well result in a SDLIC lapsing or at least a Reduced Paid Up (RPU) contract with minimal death benefit and minimal cash value remaining.

How Life Insurance Agents are Compensated

There is a mindset that permeates the world of finance that the main reason permanent cash value life insurance is sold is because licensed insurance agents get paid a lot of money. While explaining all of the benefits of SDLIC and the reasons it creates flexibility, access, and control of your money is valuable, we feel the best way to take this issue *off the table in the minds of the public* is to explain in great detail how a licensed insurance agent is compensated.

MIC's all have different contracting patterns and establish relationships with licensed agents in multiple ways. Some agents may be W-2 employees of the MIC and are normally limited to using only that company's products. Other agents may establish a 1099-Independent Contractor status with MIC's and therefore have the ability to represent multiple companies at one time. Understanding what type of relationship an agent has with the company they are recommending to you can help you analyze whether the policy design is optimal for your situation.

MIC's all compensate an agent in a similar manner with a focus on First Year commissions and Renewal commissions. First year commissions will be paid dependent on the design of the SDLIC and the mix between Base premiums and LPUA's. The Base premium is where the bulk of the first year and renewal commissions are paid. Depending on the product offered by a MIC, the standard agent compensation is 50%-60% of the base premium in the first year. Then over the next nine years (Years 2-10), the agent could be compensated an amount equal to 5%-10% of the base premium. This amount is usually higher in years two through four and lower from years five through ten. Then beyond year ten, the agent would receive a service fee equal to 1%-2% of the base premium paid as long as the policy remains in force. The agent also receives compensation for any Paid-Up Additions (LPUA or SPUA) put into the policy. This amount would equal 2%-4% of the PUA and similar to base premium compensation, the earlier the PUA is contributed to the policy, the greater the percentage in commissions paid.

Here is an example so you can see in print what the total compensation looks like for a licensed agent over the entire capitalization period (seven years):
- Annual Policy Premium $100,000
  - $30,000 Base Premium
    - Base Premium Compensation – Year 1
      - $30,000 X 55% = **$16,500**
  - $70,000 LPUA Premium
    - LPUA Premium Compensation – Year 1
      - $70,000 X 2% = **$1,400**

TOTAL FIRST YEAR COMPENSATION = $17,900

- Years 2 – 7 Compensation on $100,000 Annual Premium
  - $30,000 Base Premium
    - Base Premium Compensation – Year 2-7
      - $30,000 X 5% = **$1,500 Each Year**
  - $70,000 LPUA Premium
    - LPUA Premium Compensation – Year 2-7
      - $70,000 X 2% = **$1,400 Each Year**
  - YEARS 2-7 COMPENSATION = **$2,900 Each Year**

YEARS 2-7 COMPENSATION = $2,900 X 6 Years = $17,400

Over seven years the agent has been compensated **$35,300** to design and implement the SDLIC. Is that *too much compensation?* How do you judge whether the level of compensation is fair or not?

Let's compare this compensation to a Registered Investment Advisor who charges a client a 1% management fee to invest their money in securities. We will invest $100,000/year for seven years to keep the comparison *apples-to-apples.*

- Invest $100,000 Annually and pay a 1% management fee
  - Year 1 - $100,000 invested @1% fee = **$1,000**
  - Year 2 - $200,000 invested @1% fee = **$2,000**
  - Year 3 - $300,000 invested @1% fee = **$3,000**
  - Year 4 - $400,000 invested @1% fee = **$4,000**
  - Year 5 - $500,000 invested @1% fee = **$5,000**
  - Year 6 - $600,000 invested @1% fee = **$6,000**
  - Year 7 - $700,000 invested @1% fee = **$7,000**

Total Compensation over seven years = $28,000

Note: This number assumes no profit or loss on the invested principal or any additional fees or expenses beyond the 1% management fee. Actual results would vary and change the overall fees paid to the registered investment advisor and third party investment companies.

This comparison shows the life insurance agent was paid $7,300 more than the investment advisor over the seven year period to re-position their $700,000 into a SDLIC. That $7,300 would also equate to an average of 0.15% annually in higher compensation to the life insurance agent ($7,300/$700,000 = 1.04%/7 years = 0.149% annually).

It's also important to realize that most investment vehicles will have additional fees beyond the management fee paid to the advisor. Whether you are utilizing individual securities, exchange traded funds, index mutual funds, active mutual funds or separately managed accounts, it is fair to assume that the additional fees to one's portfolio could eclipse 0.15% in any one year.

The point we are attempting to make is that it is possible that both of these professionals can implement strategies for their clients and act in a fiduciary capacity even though their method of compensation is different. This strategy is all about adding value to the clients' personal/business economy.

It is true that MIC's will also pay additional compensation to the organization the agent is appointed with to offer the MIC's products (Agency, Brokerage Group, or Independent Marketing Organization). This compensation varies greatly and is dependent on the organization's overall production with the MIC. This compensation is used to train each agent on the proper usage of cash value life insurance as well as build systems and infrastructure to adequately serve their clients' needs. MIC's provide very little training for licensed agents and while they intend to serve all policy holders, it is much more convenient for a client to deal directly with the staff of the agent or organization that implemented the policy in the first place.

Since a properly built SDLIC uses only 30%-60% of premiums towards the base premium, a properly trained insurance agent is actually **lowering their potential compensation** to design a policy in the client's best interests. Yes, it's true that an agent will be well compensated to implement a SDLIC but it's important to note that when you view an illustration for a SDLIC all fees, expenses, and compensation for all parties are reflected in the figures. **This means the illustration is NET of all fees, expenses, and compensation.** If a licensed agent can educate you properly on this concept and shows you how you can utilize a SDLIC to take control of your financial picture, we believe a **WIN-WIN scenario** can create long term benefits for both the client and the financial professional! If the clients' needs are prioritized and the financial professional is truly acting in a fiduciary capacity, then this analysis should answer the *compensation debate* and the focus can now turn to proper capitalization of a SDLIC.

Chapter 6.   Proper Capitalization of SDLIC

When a properly trained financial professional builds a SDLIC for a client, it is accomplished by accessing three sources of capitalization:

- Excess Cash Flow
- Existing Personal Assets that are Liquid
- Existing Business Assets that are Liquid

Funding a life insurance policy in a specific way potentially optimizes the owner's income tax situation and creates access to the cash value that is substantially increased beyond normal policies.

Our intention is to analyze your sources of capital and determine how we can maximize the contract's funding in the first five to seven years. With certain mutual insurance companies, this policy design creates an accelerated level of access to your money – potentially as early as 30 days from the time you make a premium payment (depending on the company). And even though we ideally want to fund the SDLIC in 5-7 years, it is also possible to continue funding the contract well into the future.

To understand the flexibility, access, and control an owner can experience with a SDLIC, this diagram simplifies the concept:

As you can see, proper capitalization of a SDLIC results in temporary illiquidity – meaning you do not have access to all of your money right away. While most traditional life insurance policies have limited amounts of cash value in the first 5-10 years, a SDLIC can create access to 50-60% of your premiums and up to 100% access by year 7. Very few assets have the ability to generate an Internal Return through policy dividends and interest while you have the opportunity to create an External Return by investing elsewhere or utilizing your money for big ticket purchases. It is true that putting your money in a bank account gives you access to 100% of your money, but you should ask yourself "What is the cost of that decision to prioritize 100% liquidity?"

You're trading 100% liquidity for virtually no internal return (less than 1%) and once you take money out of your bank account, the money stops working for you forever.

There are three main components to a SDLIC that represent moving parts for the owner of a policy:

- Dividends and Interest
- Available Cash Value for Policy Loans
- Death Benefit

Depending on how your money is *flowing* in and out of your SDLIC (via new premiums, policy loans, or loan payments), the contract is designed to optimize your financial picture. As the diagram below illustrates, new capital/premiums create the foundation that build your dividends while paying back loans is no different than replenishing your savings in a traditional bank account.

Utilization Strategies

	New Capital/ Premiums	Policy Loans/ Utilization	Loan Payback/ Re-Save
Dividends + Interest	⬆	SAME	SAME
Available Cash Value for Policy Loans	⬆	⬇	⬆
Death Benefit	⬆	⬇	⬆

- Utilize the available cash value in the policy for any Big Ticket Items in your Personal or Business Economy for various LIFE EVENTS
- New Capital (Premiums) creates the foundation to build Dividends and Interest while paying back policy loans is no different than building your savings back up in a bank account

As soon as you contribute your first annual premium to a SDLIC, you can begin utilizing the available cash value for any big ticket need that occurs in your life. The **Common Life Events** listed below are just a few examples of events that SDLIC can assist you with over time:

Common Life Events in each Decade

- **People in their 20's**
  - Importance of Saving
  - Manage Debt
  - Purchase an Automobile
  - Cash Flow Awareness
  - Get Married
- **Clients in their 30's**
  - Start a Family
  - Purchase a Home
  - Raising Children
  - Career Decisions
  - Children's Education
- **Clients in their 40's**
  - Save MORE!
  - Upgrade/Home Improvements
  - Children's Higher Education
  - Think about Retirement

- **Clients in their 50's**
  - Plan for Retirement
  - Pay Off Home?
  - Travel/2nd Home
  - Children's Finances
- **Clients in their 60's+**
  - Get TO and THROUGH Retirement
  - Social Security/Medicare
  - Healthcare/LTC
  - More Travel
  - Grandkids/Legacy
  - Wealth Transfer/Estate Planning

Utilization strategies can be consistently optimized in your financial picture when a SDLIC is a cash flow tool made available to you. Accessing your cash value through policy loans is a very powerful and often misunderstood tool at your disposal. We have found that educating our clients about the ways traditional loans from a bank work and comparing that process to a SDLIC can demystify this strategy.

Chapter 7.   Qualification Process for a Loan from a Bank

To begin the process of making a loan with a bank, normally a borrower will contact a bank and see if they **qualify** to borrow a **certain dollar amount.** This request will cause the bank to provide a **loan application** to the prospective borrower with certain items needing to be completed. Those items will consist of the borrower's income, assets, liabilities, work history, monthly debt payments and all personal information required to do a credit check. Additional documentation will most likely be requested by the loan **underwriter** such as tax documents, pay stubs and account statements. An appraisal would also be necessary if your loan requires certain **collateral** (a car, your home, office building, equipment, etc.).

Once the underwriting process is complete, the borrower will be given an indication of approval or denial. If the loan request is approved, the bank will lay out the **terms of the loan** they choose to offer the borrower. Those terms will include the **interest rate,** the **length of the loan,** and how the payment is amortized over time (between principal and interest). Those **terms of the loan** do not provide for any **flexibility**. You can request that the length of the loan be changed (30-year vs. 15-year mortgage or 5-year vs. 3-year car loan) but that adjustment would most likely cause the bank to change the remaining terms in their favor. Normally, the longer the length of the loan is, the higher the interest rate, which causes the monthly payment to be amortized differently. The change in amortization will result in more interest being paid each month earlier in the loan. This way, the bank receives its profit sooner and your outstanding loan balance takes longer to decline.

The chart below summarizes some typical Amortization schedules for common loans made by individuals and families:

	Principal	Interest
Home Mortgage	35% Assumes 30 yr. fixed amortization with 3.5% interest	65% This percentage will decrease as future payments occur
Car Payment (Own it)	80% Assumes 5 yr. fixed amortization with 5.0% interest	20% A lot lower amount of interest to the bank but they still CONTROL your money!
Credit Card payment	10% Assumes minimum payment with a 10% interest on balance	90% At this rate it would take someone ~30 years to pay off the balance!

If you desire to **restructure** any component of your loan, this request will require the borrower to **re-qualify** and essentially start the loan process over from the beginning. Even if you don't desire to restructure your existing loan, it is possible that **life events** may cause financial stress or opportunity and force you to apply for a new loan! How many times in your lifetime will you move to a new home, buy a new vehicle, desire to perform home improvements or need access to your home equity to assist your family (kids' education, weddings, unexpected health issues, etc.)? If you own a business, how often will you need to replace old equipment, expand your office space, get access to operating capital or upgrade the technology that makes you competitive? It can be a painful process to go back to the bank every time things change in your personal or business economy.

Finally, realize that in today's economy, it is rare for a bank to loan you money based on just your ability to pay them back or your history of being a "good customer." These types of personal or **signature loans** are a thing of the past. Nowadays the most scrutinized part of the loan qualification is the assessment of your **collateral.** The bank will require that your collateral be appraised and they are in charge of choosing who appraises the collateral in most situations. Also, the bank will want the collateral to be as liquid as possible and they will make sure your loan balance does not exceed a certain percentage of the collateral. For instance, most first mortgages won't collateralize more than 80% of your home value. The terms of the first mortgage will be based on the value of your home at the time the initial loan is finalized. If your home appreciates in value, you cannot restructure the terms without a completely new application.

In summary, the qualification process for a loan with a bank has these features:
- Borrower chooses Dollar Amount to borrow
- Bank requires Borrower to Qualify for the Loan
- Bank controls the Terms of the Loan
- The Terms of the Loan are inflexible and cannot be restructured without restarting the loan qualification process
- Most bank loans require Collateral these days
- Banks want collateral that is liquid and the value is determined by appraisers normally chosen by the bank

This **structured** loan process favors the bank's financial position over the borrower. What if a more **unstructured** platform could be utilized to access capital in today's economy? Could opportunity costs be minimized for the borrower?

Chapter 8.   Qualification Process for a Loan from a Specially Designed Life Insurance Contract (SDLIC)

One of the misunderstood features with a life insurance contract is the ability to access the cash value through a **policy loan.** Here is an excerpt from the September 2014 Lara-Murphy report written by Carlos Lara, co-author of the book, *How Privatized Banking Really Works:*

In addition to bonds, the life insurance companies hold several other types of investments including mortgages, equities, real estate, cash, derivatives, and other short term investments. One such investment is the policy loan. As of 2012, the life insurance industry's aggregate assets in policy loans stood at only 3.7%. Policy loans remain a very small percentage of invested assets.[2] Mr. Lara goes on to quote a leading life insurance text book:

"Policy loans are unique among life insurance investments for two reasons. First, they are not made as the result of an investment management decision. They are options exercised at the discretion of the policy holder. Second, because loans should never exceed their cash values and unpaid principal amounts may be deducted from cash surrender or policy death proceeds, the safety of principal associated with most loans is absolute." [3]

When comparing the process of a policy loan versus a traditional loan through a bank, the terms are very favorable to the borrower when a life insurance company is the financial institution. Once a policy is funded and money is available, the policy owner can request a loan. There is no qualification process; only a loan request form must be completed noting the dollar amount and the method of payment (mailing the check or direct deposit into a checking account). The policy owner gets to decide when the loan will be repaid (if at all). The flexibility in the repayment structure is ideal because it allows the policy owner to control their personal or business economy. If cash flow is plentiful, an accelerated repayment can be set up. If cash flow is temporarily tight, then a decision to delay repayment until a future date may be appropriate. And if the policy loan is being utilized to create wealth by other means (a strategic investment or paying off

---

[2] Carlos Lara, "The Policy Loan Debate Explained," *Lara-Murphy Report,* September 2014
[3] Lara, "The Policy Loan Debate Explained"

debt), the positive leverage created by the SDLIC can lead to the policy owner benefiting from uninterrupted compound growth.

This phenomenon of uninterrupted compound growth occurs when a policy owner experiences both an internal return from policy dividends and interest while simultaneously receiving an external return in their personal/business economy. In our opinion, the best types of policies that produce uninterrupted compound growth have certain features in their product design.

1) Policy loans are made by borrowing **against** your policy's cash values, not **from** your policy's cash value. This means your policy loan is made directly with the life insurance company and you are borrowing from their general assets. This loan method does not impact the dividends paid to your policy or the compound interest earned on your policy. Essentially, your internal return is unaffected. The insurance company will hold your policy's cash surrender value and the death benefit as collateral for your loan. If you decide to surrender your policy while a loan balance exists or if you die with a policy loan, the loan balance plus interest is subtracted and the remainder is paid either to the policy owner (in the example of surrender) or the beneficiary (in the example of death).

2) The contract offers a favorable amortization when loan repayments are made. As mentioned earlier, most financial institutions will control the amortization of how much principal and interest compose each payment. However, if you have a SDLIC with an insurance company who amortizes the loan in the borrowers favor, the results can offer substantially more flexibility. Finding an insurance company that will apply a large percentage of loan repayments towards principal first means those funds are available to be accessed by the policy owner for immediate borrowing! Finding an insurance company that applies 100% of the loan repayments to principal is ideal and working with an advisor who is an expert in SDLIC can accomplish this task.

3) When a policy loan is made with an insurance company they will require collateral just like any other financial institution. However, *the insurance company is willing to accept an illiquid form of collateral – the policy death benefit*. As long as you keep your policy inforce and maintain some amount of cash surrender

value, your death benefit will be used to pay off the loan balance. The remaining death benefit will pass to your beneficiary(ies) income tax free. At this time, I think it is important to address one of the most common concerns with this strategy that involves borrowing from a life insurance policy:

Why is it a good idea to borrow my own money and pay interest on my own money (The wrong question with the right idea)?

This question is asked by the public a lot and creates confusion because the reality is very different from question! The answer to this question is rooted in both the tax code and the structure of a life insurance company.

First, you want to borrow from a life insurance company using a policy because policy loans have preferential treatment in the Internal Revenue Code (see IRC Section 7702). Technically, you are borrowing from the life insurance company's general portfolio while they are holding your cash surrender value and death benefit as collateral. So, you never touch the cash value in your policy. Through a policy loan you can access internal growth and principal without being taxed as long as the policy remains inforce.

The second thing to realize is the difference between **PAYING** interest on a loan and being **CHARGED** interest on a loan. Paying interest means the interest is already built into the amortization of your loan payment. With a policy loan, the insurance company **CHARGES** you interest and that interest is paid after your principal is prioritized. So, if an insurance company applies 100% of your loan payment to the principal balance that means your loan principal gets paid off first and the interest is the last thing to be eliminated. Whether the loan is direct recognition or non-direct recognition, the loan interest will not improve the internal return on the policy if it is paid off. So, the interest may be left to accumulate against the death benefit, so as not to interrupt access to the policy utilization while the insured is still alive.

Most Americans have been conditioned to focus on the interest rate itself versus when you are paying interest and how much over time. The benefit of the SDLIC is that the actual interest charged decreases over time when loans are paid back because that money is going to the loan balance, not paying the interest to the life insurance company. Very few financial professionals can explain this difference to you!

In order to optimize your own privatized banking, it is imperative that you customize its design to fit your cash flow, available assets, income tax situation and your utilization needs.

Chapter 9.   Life Insurance as an Asset Class

As this book is being written at the end of 2015, the stock market is near its all-time highs, yields on bonds are still close to historical lows and banks are paying less than 1 percent on savings accounts and CD's. In this environment, what is a conservative saver supposed to do? The concept of using a Specially Designed Life Insurance Contract (SDLIC) as an alternative asset class to bonds and cash is a concept taking shape in the financial services industry. Here are some reasons why we believe that a SDLIC can replace the role that traditional fixed income assets performed in your portfolio over the last 30+ years.

REASON #1

Life insurance companies (specifically mutual insurance companies - MIC) are financial institutions with unique characteristics that can offer a different way to allocate your monies versus bonds and cash. According to Carlos Lara,[4] the co-author of *How Privatized Banking Really Works*, a life insurance company plays the role of a **financial intermediary** in our economy. Their activities are similar to banks, finance companies, mutual funds, and hedge funds because they create their own financial products and act as a custodian with funds received by the account holders. Each of these companies invest those monies received into **primary securities** such as stocks, bonds, mortgages, or real estate.

Mr. Lara explains that these financial intermediaries can allow individuals, families and business owners the ability to diversify their portfolios without the need to do a substantial amount of research and due diligence. Facilitating the flow of information helps the intermediary reduce transaction costs for the customer. Life insurance companies have been acting as a financial intermediary for hundreds of years. They take in large sums of money from the public every year and as of year-end 2012, life insurance companies held $5.6 Trillion in financial assets compared to $15 Trillion in assets held by banks. What makes a life insurance company unique is that their operation is more of a **liability driven business** with actuarial certainties already factored into their financial models. The main financial product offered to the public, a life insurance contract, provides protection through the death benefit as well as the accumulation of savings.

---

[4] Lara, "The Policy Loan Debate Explained"

Because both the death benefit and cash value of the policy are a liability on the insurance company's financials, it is very important that the assets held on their books represent a conservative portfolio. Looking at data provided by SNL Financial[5], the life insurance industry aggregate assets accomplish this goal:

Bonds -	74.8% (mainly corporate bonds)
Equities -	2.3%
Mortgages -	9.9%
Real Estate -	0.6%
Policy Loans -	3.7%
Cash and Short Term Investments -	3.1%
Derivatives -	1.2%
Other Investments -	4.4%
TOTAL ASSETS -	100%

Since almost three-fourths of life insurance companies' assets are held in bonds, it is important to address a concern most people mention: *Wait, I thought you said investing in bonds was a bad idea in today's economy? Why would I want to put money in a financial institution that has most of their assets in bonds?*

BUYING POWER
First thing to understand when investing is **size matters.** The larger your portfolio or the more money you have to invest, finding better opportunities with more attractive terms is a possibility. Who do you think will get access to better yielding bonds: an individual with $500,000 to invest OR an insurance company with $50 million to invest? If a corporation can sell a bigger chunk of its debt offering to an investor willing to buy $10 million worth of bonds, the corporation may be willing to pay an extra 0.5% to 1% on the offering versus rounding up 1,000 investors at $10,000 each.

INSTITUTIONAL ASSET MANAGEMENT
The second thing to realize is that a life insurance company has a unique structure to its portfolio that is very different from individual investors. The main risk to a life insurance company is actuarial in nature, not market related. This means that as long as the people insured as a risk pool live to their normal mortality, the life insurance company has already accounted for the major costs in their financial models. The fluctuation of their underlying investments in their

---

[5] Lara, "The Policy Loan Debate Explained"

portfolios (again, mostly bonds) will not impact the long term solvency of their balance sheet. This is because a life insurance company has a huge advantage over individual investors when designing their portfolio. The life insurance company is receiving an annual stream of new money to invest from the policy premiums. This fact allows them to maintain a long term focus on their portfolios while also being able to adjust to economic changes.

Both individual investors and life insurance companies want to generate growth through income and appreciation but a life insurance company's **time horizon** is much longer than most individuals (especially mutual insurance companies). Individuals will be impacted by an increasing interest rate environment because their bonds are mostly held in mutual funds and not individually issued bonds. Mutual insurance companies are adequately prepared for interest rate changes and their asset management tool relates to the dividend rate they pay to policy holders. As interest rates have fallen since the early 1980's, so have the rate of dividends paid by MIC's. But as interest rates move higher, dividend rates have the potential to move in that same direction. The positive correlation between interest rates and dividends is a huge benefit to individuals, families and business owners thinking about SDLIC. If we see interest rates rise in the future, then dividends could increase regardless of how one is utilizing the cash value in a SDLIC contract.

FINANCIAL STRENGTH
It is often mentioned by people who have money sitting in the bank, that one of the main reasons they want their money in the bank is **safety.** The perceived safety is directly related to FDIC protection on one's bank account up to $250,000. The Federal Deposit Insurance Corporation (FDIC) is a US government corporation operating as an independent agency created by the Banking Act of 1933. As of August 27, 2014 the FDIC insured deposits at 6,638 institutions. FDIC is funded by premiums that banks and thrift institutions pay for deposit insurance coverage and from earnings on investments in US Treasury securities.

FDIC pools its reserves into the Deposit Insurance Fund (DIF). When people deposit or save money in a bank, they are under the impression that their money has *FDIC protection*. It is important to know what assets are actually backing their bank's assets should the bank fail for some reason. At the end of 2007, the DIF had a balance of $52.4 Billion on insured deposits of $4.29 Trillion. That represents a reserve ratio of 1.22%. The fund is mandated by law to keep a balance in the DIF equivalent to 1.15% of insured deposits.[6] That ratio is extremely low compared to reserve requirements for other types of financial institutions and that is why the FDIC also reminds depositors on their website www.fdic.gov that *FDIC deposit insurance is backed by the full faith and credit of the United States government*. What that essentially tells you is the US government will use all of its powers to tax and spend to protect depositors. Of course, it is ironic that the people being affected by higher taxes and loss of purchasing power through currency devaluation are the same people depositing more of their savings into banks! Finding another financial institution that values financial strengths as one of its main purposes is paramount for conservative savers today.

Life insurance companies are overseen by each state they do business in. Each state has a state-sponsored Guaranteed Insurance Fund (GIF). A portion of each insurance company's revenue generated in that particular state is paid into the fund as a "premium" similar to how banks pay a premium to the FDIC. This is one method that policy holders receive safety because if an insurance company ever became insolvent, the GIF would look to provide the contractual guarantees in existing policies while other insurance companies consider possible acquisitions of the troubled insurance company's assets. High quality life insurance companies focus on multiple areas of strength when looking at their balance sheet. **Risk Based Capital (RBC)** measures the minimum amount of capital for a company to support their overall business operations. A good company will be in the 7%-10% RBC range and a great company will have a 10%+ RBC. Another method of measuring strength deals with the analysis of ratings agencies. Ratings agencies like Standard & Poors and Moody's will regularly monitor the financial strength of life insurance companies. Dealing with at least an "A" rated company is our recommendation because that means they are well positioned for changes in almost any economic climate. And the last tool to gauge the strength of life insurance companies is the **Comdex Score**. The Comdex is a combination of several industry variables used to "grade" a company on a scale of 0-100. Our recommendation is to deal with companies with a score of 90 or above.

---

[6] Investopedia, The History of the FDIC, http://www.investopedia.com/articles/economics/09/fdic-history.asp

Dealing with a financial professional who has done their due diligence on several mutual insurance companies is important. You want to understand the reasons behind choosing a company and how their operations will sustain over the long term through multiple economic cycles.

REASON #2
The purpose of most fixed income investments inside of a portfolio is to minimize risks associated with equity securities and fulfill the need of generating income off your portfolio. We have mentioned before that ever since the 1980's, holding bonds and cash in your portfolio did an amazing job of reducing risk and generating growth in your portfolio. The concern we have is this: *What happens from today (2015) forward - knowing that most people's time horizon for saving and utilizing money is at least 30-40 years?*

With interest rates at historical lows and banks having no need or desire to pay savers anything on their bank accounts, it's time to "think differently" about risk minimization strategies. A SDLIC has the characteristics to accomplish your **Utilization strategies** while minimizing the key risks that threaten your personal economy:

Market Volatility
The uncertainty of the market is a big reason there are so many assets sitting in investments tied to bonds and cash. Even while stocks produce solid, long term returns, history has shown that stocks don't always go up over certain time periods (1960's, 1970's, and 2000's). The benefit of SDLIC is that it doesn't rely on stock market performance at all to accomplish its intended results. As mentioned before, life insurance companies on average have less than 3% of their assets in equities. And dividend payments are more about matching assets to liabilities over the long term while optimizing a growth through income approach. Implementing a SDLIC in your financial picture is one strategy to reduce market volatility in your portfolio.

Inflation
Some people believe that **inflation** means a rise in interest rates. While interest rate movements can be a symptom or result of inflation, the real definition should be understood as the *loss of purchasing power through the devaluation of our currency*. In order to stay ahead of inflation, one needs to utilize strategies that grow your assets at a rate above the inflation rate. That rate of growth can be created through income and appreciation sources.

With our current economic environment, it can be difficult to get a fixed income security (like a bond) or a cash account to appreciate in value. Why? Because as interest rates increase, the jump in yields will be offset by the loss in bond principal. Cash accounts just experience income through interest payments, which is set by the banks. A SDLIC is able to provide conservative savers a way to hedge inflationary concerns and its impact on your personal/business economy. As interest rates rise, dividend rates can rise to offset the negative impact on your financial picture. Since dividends are positively correlated to interest rate movements, there is a way to have your money working for you (through dividends and interest) while you also have the ability to utilize your money (through policy loans). This combination is hard to find in other asset classes.

Income Taxes
Most mutual insurance companies who offer policies that fit the SDLIC strategy are more than 100 years old. For example, one company that we utilize, Lafayette Life, has been operating since 1905. That means they are older than our Internal Revenue Code, which was established in 1913 with the creation of the Internal Revenue Service. Since the inception of our tax code, life insurance contracts have always received tax preferential treatment. For example, dividends from whole life policies are treated as a return of capital for tax purposes making those policies very tax efficient. The internal build-up of cash value in a policy grows tax deferred and is accessible by the policy owner on a tax free basis through proper use of policy loans. Finally, beneficiaries receive the death benefit income tax free. If a policy loan exists when the insured passes away, the loan balance is simply subtracted from the death benefit and the remaining balance goes to the beneficiary income tax free.

The only other assets that retain similar income tax benefits like a SDLIC are Roth IRA accounts, municipal bonds, and the equity in your personal residence (i.e. your home equity). Unfortunately, in our opinion, these other assets do not possess the same level of flexibility, access, and control that a SDLIC provides the policy owner.

Longevity Risk
As more people plan to retire, the concern over running out of money becomes a bigger reality for millions of Americans. Determining a way to take care of both your month-to-month expenses and big ticket items in retirement is essential if a retiree wants to enjoy retirement!

SDLIC's are built to manage one's big ticket items throughout retirement and all of its other benefits optimize its utilization so the purpose of one's money is protected.

REASON #3

If a SDLIC is set up with the right contract offered from a highly rated mutual insurance company, then you will own a very unique financial vehicle. SDLIC's achieve **uninterrupted compound growth** when very few asset classes have the ability to do so. It's tough for people to comprehend this concept because most people are not aware of the **opportunity costs** that relate to every financial decision. When you choose to do something with your money (save it, spend it, or invest it), the opportunity cost relates to the fact that your money could always be doing something else. Consider these examples:

Example #1

You are contemplating a big ticket purchase of a car. It will cost you $30,000 to buy the car but you don't have that amount of money saved at this time. You have the option of financing the car and making $525 monthly payments (five year loan at 1.99%). After careful analysis of your cash flow, a decision is made to hold off on buying the vehicle until you have saved up enough money to pay cash.

The opportunity cost in this example is that by choosing to pay cash for the vehicle, you will not own a new car for the next 3-5 years (depending on the amount you save each month towards a car purchase).

Example #2

There is $100,000 sitting in your savings account at the bank. It is earmarked for major expenses that occur throughout your lifetime. You add money to this account every so often when you're checking account balance gets too high or when you have a financial windfall (commission check, tax refund, RMD withdrawal from your IRA, etc.). At one time you were earning 5% on the balance in this account but now you only receive 0.5% on this account. Two things bother you about the current situation with this account:

#1 – You are earning 90% less interest (5% vs. 0.5%) on the account balance but you do not want to risk losing the principal by putting the money in an investment.

Opportunity cost – Choosing a low interest rate over the risk of principal loss.

#2 – Whenever you use the money in this account for big ticket items (pay cash for a car, go on a vacation, pay your taxes, fix up your house, etc.), you worry about the uncertainty of your future. You think to yourself – "What happens if I need that money in 20 years because my health deteriorates?"

Opportunity cost – Once you use your money sitting in your savings account, it is considered gone forever. Whether you are making 5% or 0.5%, all of that interest you *could have* earned in the future will be lost!

#3 – You are a conservative investor and you have done well for yourself by saving and accumulating money in different asset classes, including stock, bonds, cash, real estate and various business ventures. You have built up a pool of money that you do not need for your month-to-month expenses ($500,000) and you have invested those particular dollars into municipal bonds paying a 4% tax free yield.

One of your former business partners approaches you with a business opportunity that requires a sizeable cash investment - $100,000. After reviewing the details of this opportunity, you are confident that your skill set could be beneficial to the success of this opportunity. If the investment pays off, the cash flow generated could equate to 20% of your invested principal with realistic assumptions. The question is: *Do you liquidate $100,000 of your muni bond portfolio to invest in this business opportunity?*

Opportunity cost – In order to potentially achieve 20% cash flow from your $100,000 investment, you need to give up the 4% yield on your muni bonds and put your investment principal in a situation where the loss of principal is greater. You are faced with giving up a known return and apparent safety of principal for something that is unknown with greater growth potential. Depending on your mindset with money or finance related decisions, opportunity costs can result in more of **your money flowing out of your control** and into the control of other financial institutions. With the implementation of a SDLIC, your personal/business economy has the ability to optimize the internal, external, and eternal returns of your financial picture.

Chapter 10.   Explanation of a SDLIC Illustration

The partial illustrations that follow are designed to show you the specifics of SDLIC and to also distinguish SDLIC from traditional permanent life insurance designs. As you will see, the figures support our contention that SDLIC can effectively be utilized in a personal or business economy as an alternative asset class replacing cash and/or bonds in a portfolio.

Each illustration is based on a male who is 50 years old and who qualifies at a standard health rating. There is no particular reason a 50-year-old male was chosen. This strategy can be used at almost any age as long as the person is relatively healthy when compared to the rest of the population. When we build a SDLIC, the sex, age, and dollars contributed won't change the overall results in a proportionate sense. However, there are a few characteristics that will impact certain components of the design:

- Insuring a female versus a male will normally create a little more long-term cash value and a slightly higher death benefit.

- The younger the insured, the higher the total death benefit for the same amount of premium and a slightly higher cash value in the long term. This is because the younger the insured, the longer the insurance company will have to pay dividends and interest on the policy. This creates a slightly higher cash value beyond Year 20 in the policy.

- The healthier the insured is deemed by the underwriters, the more flexibility in your SDLIC. Cash value will be improved for a healthier client beyond Year 20 of the policy. If an insured does have health issues but still receives an offer from the insurance company, a well-trained financial professional may still be able to design a SDLIC to function appropriately. Each client situation is unique.

- For the same amount of premium, the older the insured, the greater the percentage of net cash value is made up of dividends. This is because the older the insured, the shorter someone's life expectancy and that means less years for the insurance company to pay dividends. So, dividends will be higher earlier in the policy the older the insured but the overall cash value will not be much different until you get beyond Year 20 in the policy.

Certain areas of the illustrations are purposely highlighted to draw your attention to those sections. Those highlighted areas will be explained in an attempt to simplify the concept in the mind of the reader. It is our belief that the numbers and illustrative models can *support* the reasons for an individual, family, or business owner to implement SDLIC. However, *the most important elements to SDLIC become apparent to someone when the strategy is customized and utilized based on the specifics of your financial situation.* It is impossible to illustrate specific scenarios that will occur in the future regarding your financial decision, either because of software limitations or differences in timing. For example, it is impossible to illustrate someone taking a policy loan in a year and then beginning a monthly payback in order to illustrate the minimization of opportunity costs. The life insurance companies' software programs only allow us to illustrate "net activity" in a year's time. These limitations only increase the value of consistent communication between clients and SDLIC trained financial professionals. Even if clients have similar goals and uses for their money, the timing, dollar amounts, ages, family dynamics, and beliefs regarding money will produce unique scenarios within each and every client's financial picture.

Use the information in this Appendix as a guide to further your understanding and comprehension of SDLIC. Ultimately, any decision to implement this strategy for you must result after several meetings with a SDLIC trained financial professional. The more people that read this book, talk with their friends, family, and colleagues about this concept as well as the more financial professionals who embrace this strategy, the sooner the response to the comments of **Why haven't I heard of this before?** and **This sounds too good to be true!** will be **You need to read a copy of this book!**

The first illustration shows a model of SDLIC built with these parameters:
- Insured: 50 year old Male with Standard health
- Annual Premium: $50,000 for seven years
- Initial Face Amount: $510,361

There are several key elements to this page of the illustration I want to point out. First, when viewing a whole life insurance illustration, realize that the insurance company must illustrate the policy guarantees separately from non-guaranteed assumptions (like dividends and interest earned). Here, the contractual guarantees are listed on the left side of the page and non-guaranteed figures include guarantees plus dividends and interest. When an illustration says *100% of Current Dividend Scale* that means these numbers reflect the current dividends paid in 2015 will be the same for the entire illustration. How realistic is that assumption? It really depends on the future of what comprises a policy dividend: mortality experience, portfolio return of an insurance company's assets, and the stability of the company's expense management. It is our opinion that in today's economic environment, the probability that the illustration's dividend scale will be the same or better over the next 10-20-30 years is strong. The reasons are simple. Barring any new medical epidemic that could dramatically change human's life expectancies, we believe medical science will continue to improve people's life spans. Right now, a 50-year-old male can expect to live until Age 80. In 1995, it was 72.5 and in 1985 it was 71.1 years. People are living longer and that is financially beneficial to the owners of a mutual insurance company (i.e. the policy holders).

Next, consider that interest rates are currently at or near all-time lows. The 10-year US Treasury Note is yielding in the 2.2% range, 20-year US Treasury Bond is around 2.6% and the 30-year US Treasury Bond was near 3% (September 2015). There is a high likelihood that interest rates will increase in the future. If this occurs, a mutual insurance company's portfolio will benefit and they would be able to increase dividend rates over time.

Finally, most of the mutual insurance companies who offer products that fit SDLIC requirements are very old and conservative financial institutions. It is very common to work with a company who has been in business for 100+ years and focus heavily on minimizing expenses and containing costs because management is very aware that the best way to benefit their shareholders (i.e. policy holders) is through policy dividends. As we mentioned earlier in the book, the SDLIC strategy is funded with surplus cash flow or existing assets over a five to seven year period. In this illustration we show $50,000 being funded into the policy over seven years and then no more new premiums. This type of design is optimal for the purpose of building both immediate accessibility to the cash value as well as long-term accumulation with tax-free access to your money through policy loans. There are several *behind the scenes* elements to a SDLIC that very few clients or financial professionals realize.

Sentinel 15: Level Premium Whole Life Insurance Policy
Tabular Detail

Age 50 Male
Standard No Tobacco
Dividend Option: PUA
Riders: TLR LPUA ABR

Initial Annual Premium: $50,000
Initial Face Amount: $510,361

		Guaranteed			Non-Guaranteed Assumptions 100% of Current Dividend Scale					
Age	Year	Contract Premium	Net Cash Value	Death Benefit	Premium Outlay	Surrender to Pay Premium	Annual Dividend	Increase in Net Cash Value	Net Cash Value	Death Benefit
51	1	50,000	32,013	868,961	50,000	0	9,806	41,819	41,819	878,768
52	2	50,000	69,766	925,666	50,000	0	10,112	48,191	90,010	963,104
53	3	50,000	108,214	980,549	50,000	0	10,446	49,559	139,569	1,045,594
54	4	50,000	147,372	1,033,687	50,000	0	12,296	52,472	192,042	1,127,859
55	5	50,000	187,225	1,085,152	50,000	0	12,827	54,109	246,150	1,210,953
56	6	50,000	227,769	1,135,024	50,000	0	13,404	55,802	301,952	1,292,838
57	7	50,000	269,013	1,183,374	50,000	0	14,028	57,571	359,523	1,373,660
58	8	0	277,246	619,960	0	0	4,184	15,187	374,710	832,731
59	9	0	285,647	619,960	0	0	4,424	15,778	390,488	842,327
60	10	0	294,196	619,960	0	0	4,687	16,374	406,862	852,192
61	11	0	302,857	619,960	0	0	4,999	16,976	423,838	862,380
62	12	0	311,598	619,960	0	0	5,371	17,604	441,442	872,984
63	13	0	320,371	619,960	0	0	5,788	18,216	459,658	884,087
64	14	0	329,180	619,960	0	0	6,209	18,848	478,506	895,708
65	15	0	338,021	619,960	0	0	6,633	19,484	497,990	907,826
66	16	0	346,911	619,960	0	0	7,024	20,121	518,111	920,382
67	17	0	355,870	619,960	0	0	7,389	20,768	538,880	933,299
68	18	0	364,921	619,960	0	0	7,736	21,442	560,321	946,517
69	19	0	374,065	619,960	0	0	8,044	22,085	582,406	959,968
70	20	0	383,290	619,960	0	0	8,378	22,741	605,147	973,633
71	21	0	392,565	619,960	0	0	8,760	23,403	628,551	987,567
72	22	0	401,821	619,960	0	0	9,242	24,062	652,612	1,001,883
73	23	0	410,996	619,960	0	0	9,797	24,699	677,312	1,016,697
74	24	0	420,110	619,960	0	0	10,309	25,327	702,639	1,031,987
75	25	0	429,174	619,960	0	0	10,804	25,964	728,603	1,047,696
76	26	0	438,182	619,960	0	0	11,304	26,597	755,199	1,063,802
77	27	0	447,103	619,960	0	0	11,839	27,214	782,414	1,080,331
78	28	0	455,888	619,960	0	0	12,455	27,828	810,242	1,097,363
79	29	0	464,462	619,960	0	0	13,178	28,417	838,658	1,115,023
80	30	0	472,788	619,960	0	0	13,959	28,993	867,652	1,133,394
81	31	0	480,841	619,960	0	0	14,768	29,547	897,199	1,152,508
82	32	0	488,603	619,960	0	0	15,559	30,042	927,240	1,172,339
83	33	0	496,105	619,960	0	0	16,307	30,543	957,783	1,192,828
84	34	0	503,340	619,960	0	0	17,056	31,024	988,807	1,213,955
85	35	0	510,271	619,960	0	0	17,806	31,422	1,020,229	1,235,713
86	36	0	516,848	619,960	0	0	18,519	31,670	1,051,899	1,258,059
87	37	0	523,036	619,960	0	0	19,242	31,834	1,083,733	1,280,995
88	38	0	528,814	619,960	0	0	19,577	31,549	1,115,282	1,304,138
89	39	0	534,170	619,960	0	0	19,887	31,184	1,146,466	1,327,399
90	40	0	539,093	619,960	0	0	20,172	30,737	1,177,203	1,350,765
91	41	0	543,668	619,960	0	0	20,429	30,420	1,207,622	1,374,220
92	42	0	547,983	619,960	0	0	20,670	30,255	1,237,877	1,397,757
93	43	0	552,037	619,960	0	0	20,867	30,026	1,267,903	1,421,339
94	44	0	555,825	619,960	0	0	21,045	29,745	1,297,648	1,444,951
95	45	0	559,322	619,960	0	0	21,132	29,295	1,326,943	1,468,512
96	46	0	562,583	619,960	0	0	21,356	29,092	1,356,036	1,492,159
97	47	0	565,701	619,960	0	0	21,608	29,125	1,385,160	1,515,945

This is an illustration only, not an offer, policy, contract, or promise of future policy performance. Coverage is subject to the terms and conditions of the policy. This illustration is not valid without all 11 pages.

On page 64, it breaks down the actual $50,000 premium into three parts:

- Base Policy: $27,502.53
- 10-year Term Rider ($300,000): $849
- Level Premium Paid-Up Additions Rider: $21,648.47

Each of these components of the total premium has a very specific role with SDLIC. The BASE PREMIUM (BP) is the core piece to any whole life contract. BP is what drives the long-term dividend scale of a contract while also building up the majority of your policy's death benefit. The BP does not generate any significant cash value in a policy for 10-15 years and for this reason cannot be the only component in a SDLIC. For decades insurance agents who have sold whole life policies to consumers have designed those policies almost exclusively with base premium. Because of this design, many people have a negative perception to whole life insurance as a financial vehicle.

The second important component to the premium design is the Level Premium Paid-Up Additions Rider (LPUA). In this design the LPUA is 43+% of the total premium ($21,648.47/$50,000). The LPUA Rider provides the contract with access to cash value immediately while also supporting growth of the dividend scale (to a lesser degree than the base premium). Because the LPUA rider is added at a level of 40+% the policy has $32,013 of Guaranteed Net Cash Value available to the policyholder. Based on this particular insurance company's rules, roughly 60% of the first year's premium is available in a policy loan within 30 days of receiving the $50,000.

Also, in the SDLIC, we accelerate the growth of the policy's cash value by reinvesting the dividends back into the policy to purchase more LPUAs. Each dividend is paid on the policy anniversary date. The one exception is the first year's dividend, which is paid once the second year's premium is received. As dividends are earned, they are used to purchase "mini-insurance policies" in the form of LPUAs. These single-pay contracts are added to the policy's total death benefit and they will receive a dividend of their own on the anniversary date. The "stacking" of these dividends and the death benefit causes internal compounding to take place. Once the dividends are added to the policy, they are guaranteed to not lose value and are accessible to the policyholder. At the end of the first year, you can see that $41,819 of the $50,000 annual premium is accessible to the client. That's 83% access in the first 13 months of the policy. On page 61, you can see the access percentages in the first years are as follows:

	Premiums	Cash Value	Percentage
Year 1	$50,000	$41,819	83%
Year 2	$100,000	$90,010	90%
Year 3	$150,000	$139,569	93%
Year 4	$200,000	$192,042	96%
Year 5	$250,000	$246,150	98%
Year 6	$300,000	$301,952	100%
Year 7	$350,000	$359,523	102%

As you can see, the access to the cash value in this particular SDLIC illustration is more accelerated than the charts provided to you earlier in this book. This particular product is relatively new and the mutual insurance company who brought it to the marketplace is only allowing a select number of financial professionals to offer it to their clients. The reason we wanted to share these figures in our book is to prove that there are financial institutions that are willing to provide consumers with financial vehicles that protect their personal or business economies!

The last component to the policy premium is the 10-year Term Rider. In this illustration, $300,000 of 10-year Term is being added to the contract at a cost of $849/year. Why are we adding term coverage to a permanent contract? We add the term coverage to avoid this policy design from becoming a Modified Endowment Contract (MEC). In order to protect the income tax advantages of SDLIC, there needs to be a certain amount of life insurance in force at the beginning when the policy is used until you complete seven full years of ownership Because of our design, this illustration says this policy would not be a MEC. So the amount of death benefit in force is a very key element to this strategy. Each of these three components to the premium contribute differently to the death benefit. The base premium contributes the most of the $878,768 death benefit in Year 1. The initial Face Amount of $510,361 is created by the base premium. Add in the $300,000 of term and all that is left is $68,407 ($878,768 - $810,361). This tells us that the LPUA premium of $21,648.47 purchased an additional $68,407 of permanent life insurance or 3.16x the LPUA premium. This type of financial leverage is amazing because the mutual insurance company will give you immediate access to the LPUA cash value and simultaneously creates 3x the amount of death benefit for you to use as collateral for policy loans!

Sentinel 15: Level Premium Whole Life Insurance Policy
Additional Information

Age 50 Male	Initial Annual Premium: $50,000
Male Age 50 Standard No Tobacco	Initial Face Amount: $510,361
Dividend Opt: PUA	
Riders: TLR LPUA ABR	

It is projected that on policy year 7 the election to have reduced paid up insurance has been exercised. At this point no more premiums are due. The amount of paid up insurance illustrated is dependent, in part, on non-guaranteed dividends. The actual amount of insurance may be lower or higher.

Life Insurance Cost Information

	Net Payment Cost Index		Surrender Cost Index	
	Guaranteed	Projected	Guaranteed	Projected
Year 10	46.38	28.87	26.41	8.90
Year 20	34.58	19.76	22.67	7.85

These indices are computed by the formulae as prescribed by the National Association of Insurance Commissioners, and reflect the time value of money at 5%. These indices do not include the cost of additional benefits.

Premium Information
Premiums in this illustration are assumed to be paid on a(n) Annual basis.

First Year Premiums

Regularly Billed Premiums
Paid Annual

Base Policy		$27,502.53
10 Year Term Rider(ICC14LLR-01 1408 IO)	$300,000	$849.00
Accelerated Benefit Rider(ABR-92)		$0.00
Level Premium Paid-up Additions Rider(ICC14 LLR-03 1408)		$21,648.47
Underwritten Annual LPUA Premium	$21,648.47	
Max LPUA Premium: Years 8+	$21,648.47	

$50,000.00

The initial 7-pay premium for the policy as illustrated is $50,000.03 per year. The policy, as illustrated, is not a MODIFIED ENDOWMENT CONTRACT (MEC).

Underwriting Requirements

Primary Insured Underwriting Requirements ($1,026,846):
- o Paramedical examination
- o Blood profile required including a urine specimen. Recommend an 8 hour fast before blood draw. Get special state authorization signed if state requires it.
- o 12-Lead Testing EKG (without interpretation). Use company authorized M.D. if possible.
- o Financial Supplement Form 1277 is required.

These items will be ordered by the Home Office.
- o Prescription record check
- o Database query of financial and employment records.
- o Motor Vehicle Report

Additional Information

This is an illustration only, not an offer, policy, contract, or promise of future policy performance. Coverage is subject to the terms and conditions of the policy. This illustration is not valid without all 11 pages.

As more premiums are added to the contract, the death benefit increases substantially. Over the first seven years, there is a $494,892 increase in the death benefit ($1,373,660 - $878,768). Then in Year 8, we illustrate something in the policy that few people are aware exists as an option. It is called the Reduced Paid-Up (RPU) option. What actually happens is the insurance company calculates the amount of permanent life insurance you would own if you decided to make no more premium payments. At the end of Year 7, $359,523 of cash value would purchase $832,731 of permanent coverage. If the RPU option is chosen, the death benefit is lowered to the new amount and future policy dividends will be lower to reflect the change. Now, the new RPU contract will operate as a fully funded policy and it will generate an internal return that is comprised of both interest and dividends.

For example, in Year 8, the illustration shows the new policy design increases the cash value by $15,187 even though the policy dividend in that year is only $4,184. The rest of the growth is earned interest. This policy generates a 4.22% internal rate of return ($15,187 / $359,523) in year 8. If accomplished properly, the client has income access to almost $360,000 and a paid up death benefit of $832,731 without any income tax liability. But the focus of SDLIC is not on accumulation or the death benefit. Our intention with this illustration is to educate you on SDLIC's flexibility and access to your money.

While we normally illustrate a RPU option for clients and prospects, very few of our clients ever initiate that strategy because they lose the potential to keep putting new premiums into this policy.

We understand the psychology of money and people's behaviors when it comes to making a long-term commitment. If we illustrated 20 years of premiums, how would that make you feel? Even if the premiums were much lower in years 8 through 20, there would be a part of you that may hesitate to implement this strategy because the future is uncertain for you. Rather, if we illustrate money going into a SDLIC over five to seven years and also strategize where that money will come from, the odds of you being confident about this concept and implementing this strategy increase dramatically. Just remember, the illustration is meant to help explain the concept, not detail what you will actually do in your financial picture.

AGE	YEAR	PREMIUM			CASH VALUE	DEATH BENEFIT	TOTAL IRR on NET CV	ANNUAL IRR ON NET CV	TOTAL IRR on NET DB
51	1	$ 50,000			$ 41,819	$ 878,768	(16.36)%	(16.36)%	1,657.54%
52	2	$ 50,000			$ 90,010	$ 963,104	(6.81)%	(1.97)%	291.72%
53	3	$ 50,000			$ 139,569	$ 1,045,594	(3.56)%	(0.31)%	135.28%
54	4	$ 50,000			$ 192,042	$ 1,127,859	(1.62)%	1.30%	83.09%
55	5	$ 50,000			$ 246,150	$ 1,210,953	(0.52)%	1.70%	58.20%
56	6	$ 50,000			$ 301,952	$ 1,292,838	0.19%	1.96%	43.94%
57	7	$ 50,000			$ 359,523	$ 1,373,660	0.67%	2.15%	34.82%
58	8				$ 374,710	$ 832,731	1.37%	4.22%	17.69%
59	9				$ 390,488	$ 842,327	1.83%	4.21%	15.02%
60	10				$ 406,862	$ 852,192	2.16%	4.19%	13.07%
61	11				$ 423,838	$ 862,380	2.41%	4.17%	11.60%
62	12				$ 441,442	$ 872,984	2.60%	4.15%	10.45%
63	13				$ 459,658	$ 884,087	2.75%	4.13%	9.53%
64	14				$ 478,506	$ 895,708	2.87%	4.10%	8.78%
65	15				$ 497,990	$ 907,826	2.97%	4.07%	8.16%
66	16				$ 518,111	$ 920,382	3.05%	4.04%	7.63%
67	17				$ 538,880	$ 933,299	3.12%	4.01%	7.18%
68	18				$ 560,321	$ 946,517	3.17%	3.98%	6.80%
69	19				$ 582,406	$ 959,968	3.22%	3.94%	6.46%
70	20				$ 605,147	$ 973,633	3.26%	3.90%	6.16%
71	21				$ 628,551	$ 987,567	3.29%	3.87%	5.89%
72	22				$ 652,612	$ 1,001,883	3.32%	3.83%	5.66%
73	23				$ 677,312	$ 1,016,697	3.34%	3.78%	5.45%
74	24				$ 702,639	$ 1,031,987	3.36%	3.74%	5.26%
75	25				$ 728,603	$ 1,047,696	3.38%	3.70%	5.09%
76	26				$ 755,199	$ 1,063,802	3.39%	3.65%	4.93%
77	27				$ 782,414	$ 1,080,331	3.40%	3.60%	4.79%
78	28				$ 810,242	$ 1,097,363	3.41%	3.56%	4.66%
79	29				$ 838,658	$ 1,115,023	3.41%	3.51%	4.54%
80	30				$ 867,652	$ 1,133,394	3.41%	3.46%	4.43%
81	31				$ 897,199	$ 1,152,508	3.41%	3.41%	4.33%
82	32				$ 927,240	$ 1,172,339	3.41%	3.35%	4.24%
83	33				$ 957,783	$ 1,192,828	3.40%	3.29%	4.16%
84	34				$ 988,807	$ 1,213,955	3.40%	3.24%	4.08%
85	35				$ 1,020,229	$ 1,235,713	3.39%	3.18%	4.01%

The spreadsheet on page 66 takes some key numbers off the illustration from page 61 in order to calculate an internal rate of return (IRR). One of the downsides to the SDLIC strategy is that people regularly compare the concept to more traditional concept of *investing* in vehicles like stocks, bonds, mutual funds or cash. Even though we know the utilization strategies are a key "difference maker" between SDLIC and traditional bond or cash holdings, illustrating a comparable IRR will assist in the comprehension of SDLIC in the minds of individuals, families, and business owners. Again, we are not looking at the SDLIC strategy as an *investment* but more of a financial tool.

With our current low interest rate environment, conservative savers are struggling to find ways to generate a decent internal return while also providing flexibility and access to their money. With the use of a software called Truth Concepts™, this spreadsheet calculates an internal return over 20 years at 3.26%. That calculation is NET of all fees for the life insurance coverage, any commissions paid to the advisors, and should be considered an after-tax figure. Depending on the policy owner's marginal tax bracket, the taxable equivalent return is much higher. At a 28% Federal marginal rate and a 6% state tax rate, the taxable equivalent rate is 4.94% [3.26% / (100%-34%)]. As mentioned earlier in the Appendix, the 20-year US Treasury Bond is currently yielding around 2.6% BEFORE taxes. That would make the 20-year US Treasury bond's after-tax yield 1.87% (No State income taxes charged on US Treasuries). Even the Year 10 IRR on this SDLIC strategy is comparatively strong when looking at bond and cash alternatives. A 2.16% IRR in Year 10 equates to a 3.27% taxable equivalent yield. A 10-year US Treasury Note yields in the 2.2% range or 1.58% after-taxes. Most bank Certificates of Deposit (CDs) are paying 1% or less. Even if you tie up your money for 10 years in a CD, your rate would not be any higher than 2% or 1.32% net of taxes. This chart summarizes the GROSS RETURNS available in SDLIC, bonds and cash:

	10 Years	20 Years
SDLIC	3.27%	4.94%
U.S. Treasury Note/Bond	2.20%	2.60%
Cash/Long-Term CD	2.00%	2.00%

We believe this type of data strengthens our position that SDLIC is a very unique asset class. It offers an alternative for conservative savers to reallocate money from bonds and cash into SDLIC while increasing flexibility and access to your money in any economic environment.

The next set of illustrations focus on examples of utilizing the cash value through policy loans over a 35-year period. This type of example is more compelling to our clients because the benefits of SDLIC as an alternative method of banking highlights the potential of uninterrupted compound growth and the ability to reduce opportunity costs in your personal or business economy. On pages 69-71, you will see a similar illustration as to the one on pages 61 and 64 but we are now showing how money is accessed from the contract over time through policy loans and systematic re-payments to store your wealth for future use. Page 71 shows the loan activity in detail. The same amount of money goes into the policy as premiums ($350,000) and the amount of dividends earned on the policy are not impacted by the loan activity (page 69). Also, the information on page 70 indicates the exact design of base premium, LPUA rider, and term rider to the previous illustration. So, the only difference with this illustration is the UTILIZATION of the policy's cash values. Policy loans are highlighted and shown as a positive number and loan repayments (-$12,000) are shown as a negative number. The interest charged on policy loans is calculated at 5%. Any loan repayments are allocated 100% to the principal of the loan. This is important because when any loan principal is repaid, those funds are available in 30 days to be used by the policy owner. As the loan balance increases, loan interest is being compounded on the balance and is added to the loan balance on the policy's anniversary date. The loan balance is collateralized against the cash surrender value and the death benefit.

Should a policy owner decide to surrender the policy while they are alive, the loan balance would be subtracted from the cash value and the owner would receive the net difference. If a loan is outstanding on a policy at a time when the insured dies, the loan balance would be subtracted from the gross death benefit and the net difference would be paid to the beneficiary INCOME TAX FREE. The columns on page 71 that are titled *Net Cash Value* and *Net Death Benefit* reflect numbers that are **net of the loan balance.** One other column we need to explain on page 71 is *Taxable Gain on Surrender*. This column calculates the amount of taxable gain the policy owner would have to claim on their tax return **if they surrendered the policy while they were alive.** As you can see, the potential tax liability increases substantially over time and is accelerated when you implement several policy loans. But as long as you keep your policy in force during your lifetime, there will be no adverse tax consequences. There is no reason to get rid of a SDLIC if you really understand its power to help you take control of your financial picture!

Sentinel 15: Level Premium Whole Life Insurance Policy
Tabular Detail - Loan

Age 50 Male
Standard No Tobacco
Dividend Opt: PUA
Riders: TLR LPUA ABR

Initial Annual Premium: $50,000
Initial Face Amount: $510,361

		Guaranteed			Non-Guaranteed Assumptions 100% of Current Dividend Scale					
Age	Year	Contract Premium	Net Cash Value	Death Benefit	Premium Outlay	Surrender to Pay Premium	Annual Dividend	Increase in Net Cash Value	Net Cash Value	Death Benefit
51	1	50,000	32,013	868,961	50,000	0	9,806	41,819	41,819	878,768
52	2	50,000	69,766	925,666	50,000	0	10,112	48,191	90,010	963,104
53	3	50,000	108,214	980,549	50,000	0	10,446	49,559	139,569	1,045,594
54	4	50,000	147,372	1,033,687	50,000	0	12,296	52,472	192,042	1,127,859
55	5	50,000	187,225	1,085,152	50,000	0	12,827	1,609	193,650	1,158,453
56	6	50,000	227,769	1,135,024	50,000	0	13,404	65,777	259,427	1,250,313
57	7	50,000	269,013	1,183,374	50,000	0	14,028	68,044	327,472	1,341,609
58	8	0	277,246	619,960	0	0	4,184	26,185	353,657	811,677
59	9	0	285,647	619,960	0	0	4,424	27,325	380,982	832,821
60	10	0	294,196	619,960	0	0	4,687	-36,602	344,380	789,710
61	11	0	302,857	619,960	0	0	4,999	26,452	370,832	809,374
62	12	0	311,598	619,960	0	0	5,371	27,554	398,386	829,928
63	13	0	320,371	619,960	0	0	5,788	28,663	427,049	851,478
64	14	0	329,180	619,960	0	0	6,209	29,818	456,867	874,069
65	15	0	338,021	619,960	0	0	6,633	-34,098	422,769	832,604
66	16	0	346,911	619,960	0	0	7,024	28,960	451,729	853,999
67	17	0	355,870	619,960	0	0	7,389	30,049	481,778	876,197
68	18	0	364,921	619,960	0	0	7,736	31,187	512,965	899,161
69	19	0	374,065	619,960	0	0	8,044	32,317	545,281	922,843
70	20	0	383,290	619,960	0	0	8,378	-57,865	487,417	855,903
71	21	0	392,565	619,960	0	0	8,760	30,117	517,533	876,550
72	22	0	401,821	619,960	0	0	9,242	31,111	548,644	897,915
73	23	0	410,996	619,960	0	0	9,797	32,101	580,745	920,131
74	24	0	420,110	619,960	0	0	10,309	33,099	613,844	943,192
75	25	0	429,174	619,960	0	0	10,804	-57,226	556,618	875,711
76	26	0	438,182	619,960	0	0	11,304	30,597	587,215	895,819
77	27	0	447,103	619,960	0	0	11,839	31,415	618,631	916,548
78	28	0	455,888	619,960	0	0	12,455	32,239	650,869	937,990
79	29	0	464,462	619,960	0	0	13,178	33,048	683,917	960,282
80	30	0	472,788	619,960	0	0	13,959	-57,494	626,424	892,166
81	31	0	480,841	619,960	0	0	14,768	30,086	656,509	911,818
82	32	0	488,603	619,960	0	0	15,559	30,607	687,117	932,215
83	33	0	496,105	619,960	0	0	16,307	31,136	718,253	953,298
84	34	0	503,340	619,960	0	0	17,056	31,647	749,900	975,049
85	35	0	510,271	619,960	0	0	17,806	-85,523	664,377	879,861
86	36	0	516,848	619,960	0	0	18,519	26,478	690,854	897,015
87	37	0	523,036	619,960	0	0	19,242	26,382	717,236	914,499
88	38	0	528,814	619,960	0	0	19,577	25,824	743,060	931,916
89	39	0	534,170	619,960	0	0	19,887	25,173	768,233	949,167
90	40	0	539,093	619,960	0	0	20,172	24,425	792,658	966,221
91	41	0	543,668	619,960	0	0	20,429	23,792	816,451	983,048
92	42	0	547,983	619,960	0	0	20,670	23,296	839,747	999,627
93	43	0	552,037	619,960	0	0	20,867	22,720	862,466	1,015,902
94	44	0	555,825	619,960	0	0	21,045	22,074	884,540	1,031,843
95	45	0	559,322	619,960	0	0	21,132	21,240	905,780	1,047,348
96	46	0	562,583	619,960	0	0	21,356	20,634	926,414	1,062,537
97	47	0	565,701	619,960	0	0	21,608	20,244	946,657	1,077,442

This is an illustration only, not an offer, policy, contract, or promise of future policy performance. Coverage is subject to the terms and conditions of the policy. This illustration is not valid without all 13 pages.

Sentinel 15: Level Premium Whole Life Insurance Policy
Additional Information - Loan

Age 50 Male
50 Standard No Tobacco
Dividend Opt: PUA
Riders: TLR LPUA ABR

Initial Annual Premium:	$50,000.00
Initial Face Amount:	$510,361

It is projected that on policy year 7 the election to have reduced paid up insurance has been exercised. At this point no more premiums are due. The amount of paid up insurance illustrated is dependent, in part, on non-guaranteed dividends. The actual amount of insurance may be lower or higher.

Life Insurance Cost Information

	Net Payment Cost Index		Surrender Cost Index	
	Guaranteed	Projected	Guaranteed	Projected
Year 10	46.38	28.87	26.41	8.90
Year 20	34.58	19.76	22.67	7.85

These indices are computed by the formulae as prescribed by the National Association of Insurance Commissioners, and reflect the time value of money at 5%. These indices do not include the cost of additional benefits.

Premium Information
Premiums in this illustration are assumed to be paid on a(n) Annual basis.

First Year Premiums

		Regularly Billed Premiums Paid Annual
Base Policy		$27,502.53
10 Year Term Rider(ICC14 LLR-01 1408 IO)	$300,000	$849.00
Accelerated Benefit Rider(ABR-92)		$0.00
Level Premium Paid-up Additions Rider(ICC14 LLR-03 1408)		$21,648.47
Underwritten Annual LPUA Premium	$21,648.47	
Max LPUA Premium: Years 8+	$21,648.47	
		$50,000.00

The initial 7-pay premium for the policy as illustrated is $50,000.03 per year. The policy, as illustrated, is not a MODIFIED ENDOWMENT CONTRACT (MEC).

Underwriting Requirements

Primary Insured Underwriting Requirements ($1,026,846):
- o Paramedical examination
- o Blood profile required including a urine specimen. Recommend an 8 hour fast before blood draw. Get special state authorization signed if state requires it.
- o 12-Lead Testing EKG (without interpretation). Use company authorized M.D. if possible.
- o Financial Supplement Form 1277 is required.

These items will be ordered by the Home Office.
- o Prescription record check
- o Database query of financial and employment records.
- o Motor Vehicle Report

Additional Information

This is an illustration only, not an offer, policy, contract, or promise of future policy performance. Coverage is subject to the terms and conditions of the policy. This illustration is not valid without all 13 pages.

Sentinel 15: Level Premium Whole Life Insurance Policy
Supplemental Illustration - Loan

Age 50 Male
Standard No Tobacco
Dividend Opt: PUA
Riders:TLR LPUA ABR

Initial Annual Premium: $50,000.00
Initial Face Amount: $510,361

					Non-Guaranteed Assumptions					
Age	Year	Contract Premium	Partial Surrender	Loan Amt. Less Div. To Pay Loan	Loan Interest Added to Loan	Loan Balance	Net Premium Outlay	Net Cash Value	Net Death Benefit	Taxable Gain On Surrender
51	1	50,000	0	0	0	0	50,000	41,819	878,768	0
52	2	50,000	0	0	0	0	50,000	90,010	963,104	0
53	3	50,000	0	0	0	0	50,000	139,569	1,045,594	0
54	4	50,000	0	0	0	0	50,000	192,042	1,127,859	0
55	5	50,000	0	50,000	2,500	52,500	0	193,650	1,158,453	0
56	6	50,000	0	-12,000	2,025	42,525	62,000	259,427	1,250,313	1,952
57	7	50,000	0	-12,000	1,526	32,051	62,000	327,472	1,341,609	9,523
58	8	0	0	-12,000	1,003	21,054	12,000	353,657	811,677	24,710
59	9	0	0	-12,000	453	9,507	12,000	380,982	832,821	40,488
60	10	0	0	50,000	2,975	62,482	-50,000	344,380	789,710	56,862
61	11	0	0	-12,000	2,524	53,006	12,000	370,832	809,374	73,838
62	12	0	0	-12,000	2,050	43,056	12,000	398,386	829,928	91,442
63	13	0	0	-12,000	1,553	32,609	12,000	427,049	851,478	109,658
64	14	0	0	-12,000	1,030	21,639	12,000	456,867	874,069	128,506
65	15	0	0	50,000	3,582	75,221	-50,000	422,769	832,604	147,990
66	16	0	0	-12,000	3,161	66,383	12,000	451,729	853,999	168,111
67	17	0	0	-12,000	2,719	57,102	12,000	481,778	876,197	188,880
68	18	0	0	-12,000	2,255	47,357	12,000	512,965	899,161	210,321
69	19	0	0	-12,000	1,768	37)25	12,000	545,281	922,843	232,406
70	20	0	0	75,000	5,606	117,731	-75,000	487,417	855,903	255,147
71	21	0	0	-12,000	5,287	111,017	12,000	517,533	876,550	278,551
72	22	0	0	-12,000	4,951	103,968	12,000	548,644	897,915	302,612
73	23	0	0	-12,000	4,598	96,567	12,000	580,745	920,131	327,312
74	24	0	0	-12,000	4,228	88,795	12,000	613,844	943,192	352,639
75	25	0	0	75,000	8,190	171,985	-75,000	556,618	875,711	378,603
76	26	0	0	-12,000	7,999	167,984	12,000	587,215	895,819	405,199
77	27	0	0	-12,000	7,799	163,783	12,000	618,631	916,548	432,414
78	28	0	0	-12,000	7,589	159,372	12,000	650,869	937,990	460,242
79	29	0	0	-12,000	7,369	154,741	12,000	683,917	960,282	488,658
80	30	0	0	75,000	11,487	241,228	-75,000	626,424	892,166	517,652
81	31	0	0	-12,000	11,461	240,689	12,000	656,509	911,818	547,199
82	32	0	0	-12,000	11,434	240,124	12,000	687,117	932,215	577,240
83	33	0	0	-12,000	11,406	239,530	12,000	718,253	953,298	607,783
84	34	0	0	-12,000	11,376	238,906	12,000	749,900	975,049	638,807
85	35	0	0	100,000	16,945	355,852	-100,000	664,377	879,861	670,229
86	36	0	0	-12,000	17,193	361,044	12,000	690,854	897,015	701,899
87	37	0	0	-12,000	17,452	366,497	12,000	717,236	914,499	733,733
88	38	0	0	-12,000	17,725	372,221	12,000	743,060	931,916	765,282
89	39	0	0	-12,000	18,011	378,233	12,000	768,233	949,167	796,466
90	40	0	0	-12,000	18,312	384,544	12,000	792,658	966,221	827,203
91	41	0	0	-12,000	18,627	391,171	12,000	816,451	983,048	857,622
92	42	0	0	-12,000	18,959	398,130	12,000	839,747	999,627	887,877
93	43	0	0	-12,000	19,306	405,436	12,000	862,466	1,015,902	917,903
94	44	0	0	-12,000	19,672	413,108	12,000	884,540	1,031,843	947,648
95	45	0	0	-12,000	20,055	421,164	12,000	905,780	1,047,348	976,943
96	46	0	0	-12,000	20,458	429,622	12,000	926,414	1,062,537	1,006,036
97	47	0	0	-12,000	20,881	438,503	12,000	946,657	1,077,442	1,035,160
98	48	0	0	-12,000	21,325	447,828	12,000	966,417	1,092,049	1,064,246

This is an illustration only, not an offer, policy, contract, or promise of future policy performance. Coverage is subject to the terms and conditions of the policy. This illustration is not valid without all 13 pages.

The illustration on Page 71 was not meant to mimic any utilization strategies but rather show you the long-term impact of using money in your SDLIC and also structuring loan repayments over time. A summary of the activity in this illustration is listed below.

Over a 35-year Period:

MONEY IN		MONEY OUT		LOAN REPAYMENTS		YOUR MONEY
$350,000	-	$475,000	+	$288,000	=	$163,000

These figures are indicative of normal savers cash flow awareness when money is flowing in and out of their savings/money market account. If you take some time to think about the amount of money that has flowed in and out of your *savings account* you would realize that several hundreds of thousands of dollars have left your control with minimal benefit to your financial picture. Saving money for all of these big-ticket items (new cars, home improvements, education expenses, travel, real estate taxes, healthcare emergencies, etc.) and losing the chance for those dollars to build your wealth because you needed or wanted to use the money. It is this reality that many savers face now with money market accounts paying less than 1% but no real alternative place to store their wealth while they wait to use it.

Here we illustrate $350,000 of cash flow or assets capitalizing a SDLIC to build a pool of money that can be utilized at the owner's discretion. Over 35 years, we show $475,000 of policy loans being taken over time in amounts as low as $50,000 and as much as $100,000. Accessing money through policy loans can be executed at any time with any amount of money requested. As long as the proper forms are submitted, the owner will receive the funds in a timeframe of two to five business days (depending on the method of receipt). Making a loan re-payment to the policy can also be done at your discretion, whether that's monthly from your checking account or you choose to send in a check. Repaying the policy loan is no different than rebuilding your savings account when it gets too low. All savers have a certain *cushion* they like to keep in savings. For some, that amount may be as low as $5,000 and for others the number could be as high as $100,000. Some businesses might keep several million dollars in cash as a cushion based on their inventories, receivables, equipment purchases, etc.

Loan repayments of $12,000 per year were illustrated and totaled $288,000 over the 35 year time period. When you total the net activity in this illustration, you see that $163,000 of **your money** is left in the policy after 35 years. This is an important figure because the illustration emphasizes the long-term benefits of SDLIC's uninterrupted compound growth. After using your money for 35 years, your $163,000 has turned into $664,377 income tax free. That is over 4x your money! The Net Death Benefit that remains should you pass away in Year 35 is $879,861. That amount is 5.4x your money. Having a place where you can store your money safely while having access to it is a high priority for conservative savers in today's economy.

Here is another interesting item to consider. If you add the Net Death Benefit in Year 35 ($879,861) to the Outstanding Loan Balance in Year 35 ($355,852), you get a total of $1,235,713. That figure is the exact death benefit on the original illustration from Page 61. What is the significance of this tidbit? Well, it shows you that the ultimate purpose of your death benefit with a SDLIC is to act as long-term collateral for the policy loan you create. A well-structured SDLIC will build a sizeable death benefit as a secondary element to your cash value. So, over a 35-year period, this 50-year old male was able to save and utilize his money while it generated uninterrupted compound growth. And the net results from a death benefit perspective as astoundingly negligible. This illustration shows a beginning death benefit of $878,768 and the Net Death Benefit in Year 35 is $879,861. We have found that our clients enjoy the ability to use their money over their lifetime and then pass on whatever is left to their beneficiaries in a tax-efficient manner. SDLIC allows clients to accomplish this goal with flexibility, access, and control of their money.

Just as we provided you an Internal Rate of Return on the initial illustration, the next spreadsheet is designed to calculate a taxable equivalent return after factoring in the utilization of your money. Basically, we wanted to re-create the flow of money in and out of the SDLIC as represented in the *Net Premium Outlay* column on Page 71.

Over a 35 year period, the first spreadsheet on Page 66 shows an internal return of 3.39% (5.14% Taxable Equivalent). On Page 74 the spreadsheet that factors in the utilization of your money shows an internal return of 3.11%. Both of these returns are NET of all fees, expenses, cost of the life insurance, and commissions paid to a financial professionals. The difference between these two numbers is **0.28%** (3.39% - 3.11%) and this represents the **NET OPPORTUNITY COST** experienced by utilizing your money through policy loans over 35 years. This also means the **REAL** cost of borrowing money from a SDLIC is not the 5% loan rate charged

YEAR	PREMIUM	POLICY LOANS	LOANS REPAID	CASH VALUE	DEATH BENEFIT	TOTAL IRR on NET CV	ANNUAL IRR ON NET CV	TOTAL IRR on NET DB
1	$ 50,000			$ 41,819	$ 878,768	(16.36)%	(16.36)%	1,657.54%
2	$ 50,000			$ 90,010	$ 963,104	(6.81)%	(1.97)%	291.72%
3	$ 50,000			$ 139,569	$ 1,045,594	(3.56)%	(0.31)%	135.28%
4	$ 50,000			$ 192,042	$ 1,127,859	(1.62)%	1.30%	83.09%
5	$ 50,000	$ 50,000		$ 193,650	$ 1,158,453	(0.92)%	0.84%	59.12%
6	$ 50,000		$ 12,000	$ 259,427	$ 1,250,313	(0.27)%	1.48%	45.04%
7	$ 50,000		$ 12,000	$ 327,472	$ 1,341,609	0.27%	1.88%	35.85%
8			$ 12,000	$ 353,657	$ 811,677	1.06%	4.18%	18.33%
9			$ 12,000	$ 380,982	$ 832,821	1.60%	4.19%	15.50%
10		$ 50,000		$ 344,380	$ 789,710	1.92%	4.05%	13.52%
11			$ 12,000	$ 370,832	$ 809,374	2.17%	4.06%	11.99%
12			$ 12,000	$ 398,386	$ 829,928	2.38%	4.06%	10.79%
13			$ 12,000	$ 427,049	$ 851,478	2.55%	4.06%	9.81%
14			$ 12,000	$ 456,867	$ 874,069	2.69%	4.06%	9.01%
15		$ 50,000		$ 422,769	$ 832,604	2.78%	3.91%	8.36%
16			$ 12,000	$ 451,729	$ 853,999	2.86%	3.90%	7.81%
17			$ 12,000	$ 481,778	$ 876,197	2.94%	3.89%	7.34%
18			$ 12,000	$ 512,965	$ 899,161	3.00%	3.89%	6.92%
19			$ 12,000	$ 545,281	$ 922,843	3.06%	3.87%	6.56%
20		$ 75,000		$ 487,417	$ 855,903	3.09%	3.64%	6.25%
21			$ 12,000	$ 517,533	$ 876,550	3.11%	3.63%	5.97%
22			$ 12,000	$ 548,644	$ 897,915	3.14%	3.61%	5.71%
23			$ 12,000	$ 580,745	$ 920,131	3.16%	3.59%	5.49%
24			$ 12,000	$ 613,844	$ 943,192	3.18%	3.56%	5.28%
25		$ 75,000		$ 556,618	$ 875,711	3.18%	3.30%	5.09%
26			$ 12,000	$ 587,215	$ 895,819	3.19%	3.27%	4.92%
27			$ 12,000	$ 618,631	$ 916,548	3.19%	3.24%	4.77%
28			$ 12,000	$ 650,869	$ 937,990	3.19%	3.21%	4.62%
29			$ 12,000	$ 683,917	$ 960,282	3.19%	3.18%	4.49%
30		$ 75,000		$ 626,424	$ 892,166	3.18%	2.88%	4.36%
31			$ 12,000	$ 656,509	$ 911,818	3.17%	2.83%	4.25%
32			$ 12,000	$ 687,117	$ 932,215	3.16%	2.78%	4.14%
33			$ 12,000	$ 718,253	$ 953,298	3.14%	2.74%	4.04%
34			$ 12,000	$ 749,900	$ 975,049	3.13%	2.69%	3.95%
35		$ 100,000		$ 664,377	$ 879,861	3.11%	2.23%	3.86%

by the mutual insurance company, but rather the 0.28% cost that is reflected in these spreadsheets.

How is it possible for the real cost to be less than the policy loan rate charged?

This is the power of uninterrupted compound growth on you cash value over the entire 35 year period! You are borrowing **against** (not from) the cash value and the loan interest is **charged** to your policy (not paid immediately) as a liability. This liability must be paid back but you control **when and how** the loan principal and interest is paid back. It could be from your cash flow through policy loan repayments. Or you could surrender the policy while you are alive and subtract the loan balance from the cash surrender value. Or you could choose to subtract the loan balance from your death benefit when you die and your beneficiary receives the remaining net death benefit income tax free. Regardless of how the loan balance is repaid, the important element to this discussion is that YOU CONTROL the decisions within your privatized banking system!

As Chapter 8 explained, a policy loan from a SDLIC creates flexibility for the policy owner with the **terms of the loan**. The illustration on Page 71 shows that the policy loan repayments of $12,000/yr. (or $1,000/mo.) are applied 100% to the principal of the policy loan. At the same time, those loan repayments increase the amount of money available to the policy owner to borrow against over and over. This is no different than when a saver continues to add money to their bank accounts, withdraw from those accounts for big ticket items, and then replenish those accounts with new savings. Also, realize that the key factors in the difference between a policy loan from a SDLIC versus a traditional loan from a bank dramatically reduce the opportunity costs of utilizing your own privatized banking system.

After using your money for 35 years, your money still created an internal return of 3.11% in an illustration that assumes interest rates and economic conditions will remain similar for that entire 35 year period. If you were to experience any increase in interest rates in the future, there is a high likelihood that dividends and interest paid to your SDLIC would increase and your internal return would improve – even as you are using your money over that period of time! This situation presents an unique opportunity to savers to protect the purpose of their money from the risks of market volatility, inflation, and income taxes. These illustrations provide numeric support to our claims and show why we believe that building your own privatized banking system is a vital component to protecting your personal/business economy.

What are my actual life insurance costs with a SDLIC?

This is a question we hear all of the time because whole life insurance contracts are structured in a very different way compared to term insurance or universal life contracts. With the help of the Truth Concepts software, we have taken the same illustrations on Pages 66 & 74 and adjusted them to isolate a *break-even* point in our analysis.

For the first three years of this policy, the annual amount of cash value increase is less than the annual premiums paid. After three years of contributing $50,000 annually ($150,000 total), the cash surrender value is $139,569. However, starting in Year four, the policy cash value increases by more than the $50,000 premium. The net cash value growth in Year four is $52,473 ($192,042 - $139,569). This means the break-even point to calculate the real cost of the policy is in Year three. From Year four on, the illustration has positive growth in the annual internal return (See the spreadsheet on Page 77).

To calculate the actual cost of the life insurance in the first three years, we simply take the total premiums minus the cash surrender value in Year three ($150,000 - $139,569) to get a total of $10,431. This number represents the **total opportunity cost** for this SDLIC illustration and design. Going forward, the policy's cash surrender value is experiencing positive annual internal returns as the spreadsheet on Page 77 illustrates. In Year four, the returns starts at 1.30% and they increase to 2.15% by Year seven. While those returns are not stellar, we would ask you to think of any other **safe** place to store your money these days where you are earning more than 1% income tax free? Once you are past the break-even point, the efficiency of the SDLIC improves and the cash value growth accelerates. By Year eight, the annual IRR is 4.22% assuming the Reduced Paid Up (RPU) Option is chosen. If instead, the policy owner chooses to keep putting money into the policy beyond Year seven, then both the annual and total internal return would continue to improve due to the policy's efficient design. This flexibility in funding a SDLIC gives the owner an immense amount of control as they design their privatized banking system.

AGE	YEAR	PREMIUM			CASH VALUE	DEATH BENEFIT	TOTAL IRR on NET CV	ANNUAL IRR ON NET CV	TOTAL IRR on NET DB
54	4	$ 50,000			$ 192,042	$ 1,127,859	1.30%	1.30%	494.96%
55	5	$ 50,000			$ 246,150	$ 1,210,953	1.52%	1.70%	139.90%
56	6	$ 50,000			$ 301,952	$ 1,292,838	1.70%	1.96%	76.83%
57	7	$ 50,000			$ 359,523	$ 1,373,660	1.84%	2.15%	51.83%
58	8				$ 374,710	$ 832,731	2.41%	4.22%	23.55%
59	9				$ 390,488	$ 842,327	2.76%	4.21%	19.00%
60	10				$ 406,862	$ 852,192	2.99%	4.19%	15.98%
61	11				$ 423,838	$ 862,380	3.16%	4.17%	13.83%
62	12				$ 441,442	$ 872,984	3.28%	4.15%	12.22%
63	13				$ 459,658	$ 884,087	3.37%	4.13%	10.98%
64	14				$ 478,506	$ 895,708	3.44%	4.10%	10.00%
65	15				$ 497,990	$ 907,826	3.50%	4.07%	9.20%
66	16				$ 518,111	$ 920,382	3.54%	4.04%	8.54%
67	17				$ 538,880	$ 933,299	3.58%	4.01%	7.98%
68	18				$ 560,321	$ 946,517	3.61%	3.98%	7.51%
69	19				$ 582,406	$ 959,968	3.63%	3.94%	7.10%
70	20				$ 605,147	$ 973,633	3.64%	3.90%	6.74%
71	21				$ 628,551	$ 987,567	3.66%	3.87%	6.42%
72	22				$ 652,612	$ 1,001,883	3.67%	3.83%	6.14%
73	23				$ 677,312	$ 1,016,697	3.67%	3.78%	5.89%
74	24				$ 702,639	$ 1,031,987	3.68%	3.74%	5.67%
75	25				$ 728,603	$ 1,047,696	3.68%	3.70%	5.47%
76	26				$ 755,199	$ 1,063,802	3.68%	3.65%	5.29%
77	27				$ 782,414	$ 1,080,331	3.67%	3.60%	5.13%
78	28				$ 810,242	$ 1,097,363	3.67%	3.56%	4.98%
79	29				$ 838,658	$ 1,115,023	3.66%	3.51%	4.84%
80	30				$ 867,652	$ 1,133,394	3.65%	3.46%	4.72%
81	31				$ 897,199	$ 1,152,508	3.64%	3.41%	4.60%
82	32				$ 927,240	$ 1,172,339	3.63%	3.35%	4.50%
83	33				$ 957,783	$ 1,192,828	3.62%	3.29%	4.41%
84	34				$ 988,807	$ 1,213,955	3.61%	3.24%	4.32%
85	35				$ 1,020,229	$ 1,235,713	3.60%	3.18%	4.23%

YEAR	PREMIUM	POLICY LOANS	LOANS REPAID	CASH VALUE	DEATH BENEFIT	TOTAL IRR on NET CV	ANNUAL IRR ON NET CV	TOTAL IRR on NET DB
4	$ 50,000			$ 192,042	$ 1,127,859	1.30%	1.30%	494.96%
5	$ 50,000	$ 50,000		$ 193,650	$ 1,158,453	1.07%	0.84%	147.20%
6	$ 50,000		$ 12,000	$ 259,427	$ 1,250,313	1.23%	1.48%	81.72%
7	$ 50,000		$ 12,000	$ 327,472	$ 1,341,609	1.45%	1.88%	55.08%
8			$ 12,000	$ 353,657	$ 811,677	2.13%	4.18%	25.01%
9			$ 12,000	$ 380,982	$ 832,821	2.56%	4.19%	19.98%
10		$ 50,000		$ 344,380	$ 789,710	2.78%	4.05%	16.81%
11			$ 12,000	$ 370,832	$ 809,374	2.96%	4.06%	14.52%
12			$ 12,000	$ 398,386	$ 829,928	3.09%	4.06%	12.79%
13			$ 12,000	$ 427,049	$ 851,478	3.20%	4.06%	11.44%
14			$ 12,000	$ 456,867	$ 874,069	3.29%	4.06%	10.37%
15		$ 50,000		$ 422,769	$ 832,604	3.34%	3.91%	9.53%
16			$ 12,000	$ 451,729	$ 853,999	3.39%	3.90%	8.82%
17			$ 12,000	$ 481,778	$ 876,197	3.43%	3.89%	8.23%
18			$ 12,000	$ 512,965	$ 899,161	3.46%	3.89%	7.71%
19			$ 12,000	$ 545,281	$ 922,843	3.49%	3.87%	7.26%
20		$ 75,000		$ 487,417	$ 855,903	3.50%	3.64%	6.89%
21			$ 12,000	$ 517,533	$ 876,550	3.50%	3.63%	6.55%
22			$ 12,000	$ 548,644	$ 897,915	3.51%	3.61%	6.25%
23			$ 12,000	$ 580,745	$ 920,131	3.51%	3.59%	5.98%
24			$ 12,000	$ 613,844	$ 943,192	3.51%	3.56%	5.74%
25		$ 75,000		$ 556,618	$ 875,711	3.51%	3.30%	5.52%
26			$ 12,000	$ 587,215	$ 895,819	3.50%	3.27%	5.32%
27			$ 12,000	$ 618,631	$ 916,548	3.49%	3.24%	5.14%
28			$ 12,000	$ 650,869	$ 937,990	3.47%	3.21%	4.97%
29			$ 12,000	$ 683,917	$ 960,282	3.46%	3.18%	4.82%
30		$ 75,000		$ 626,424	$ 892,166	3.44%	2.88%	4.68%
31			$ 12,000	$ 656,509	$ 911,818	3.42%	2.83%	4.55%
32			$ 12,000	$ 687,117	$ 932,215	3.40%	2.78%	4.43%
33			$ 12,000	$ 718,253	$ 953,298	3.38%	2.74%	4.32%
34			$ 12,000	$ 749,900	$ 975,049	3.36%	2.69%	4.21%
35		$100,000		$ 664,377	$ 879,861	3.33%	2.23%	4.11%

But how much life insurance does your $10,431 actually purchase? In order to calculate the amount of paid up life insurance you have purchased, we need to look at Year eight of the illustration on Page 61 or Page 66.

As mentioned previously, in this illustration we executed the Reduced Paid Up (RPU) option so that in Year eight no more annual premiums would be required. With the RPU option, the insurance company reduces the death benefit to the least amount of coverage required for the IRS to allow the tax advantages of the SDLIC to be maintained. The RPU option caused the death benefit to decrease from $1,373,660 in Year seven to $832,731. If the insured died in Year eight, a tax free death benefit would be paid to the beneficiary but that is not technically the amount of pure life insurance that you own. To calculate the amount of life insurance you own, you need to understand about the insurance company's **Net Amount at Risk**.

To figure out the Net Amount at Risk (NAR), you subtract the death benefit from the cash surrender value in any one year. In Year eight, the NAR is $457,021 ($832,731 - $374,710). The longer the insured lives, the **lower** the NAR figure becomes. Because we build the SDLIC to focus on the cash value growth, as time goes on, the death benefit is not increasing as quickly as the cash value. By Year 20 the NAR is $368,486 ($973,633 - $605,147) and in Year 35 the NAR is $215,484 ($1,235,713 - $1,020,229). Is this a *good deal* from the insurance company?

Consider that if this 50 year old male with standard health contributed $50,000 annually for seven years to this SDLIC and passed away when he was Age 85, his beneficiary would have received $215,484 of permanent life insurance coverage for a **net cost** of $10,431. If you amortize that cost over the 35 year period, it equals a cost of less than $300 annually or $25/mo. AND don't forget that he also had the $350,000 of premiums growing in a financial vehicle that earned 3+% income tax free **while those dollars were able to be utilized!** In comparison, a 30 year term policy with a $215,000 death benefit for a 50 year old male in standard health would cost $120+/mo. and you would not have a place to store your safe money to protect it from income taxes and inflation!

What If I Don't Need Life Insurance?

We understand that everyone's financial situation is unique and the purchase of life insurance is viewed by most Americans as an expense or a cost. You may think of life insurance as a *necessary evil* or something that the insured *doesn't benefit from because it is paid upon their death!*

Our hope in sharing this analysis is that you start **thinking differently** as to the benefits and flexibility of whole life insurance – especially a SDLIC created for your own privatized banking system. Instead of thinking whether or not you *need* life insurance, what if you asked yourself: *Do I want the benefits and features a SDLIC can provide me?*

For the cost of ~$300 per year (in this example) you are able to create your own privatized banking system that becomes the core financial tool to protect your personal/business economy. It is with this type of knowledge, a properly trained financial professional can guide you through the customization of your own SDLIC. We believe taking control of your financial picture will awaken the inner-entrepreneur in you and simplify your financial life.

What are my next steps?

If this book has opened your eyes to the value of what a Privatized Banking System can do to protect your personal/business economy, then your next step should be to contact the financial professional who gave you this book! If you purchased this book online or though other avenues, then reach out to e3 ConsultantsGROUP (see Page 5) and one of our financial professionals can guide you through the process of analyzing your financial picture. Remember, this strategy is not an all-in-one cure for your financial life. You need to use the Privatized Banking System as a tool to make your financial picture more efficient! Let a properly trained financial professional be your guide on this journey. Thank you for taking the time to read this book. We wish you luck in thinking differently about your money and finance related decisions.

WORKS CITED

Investopedia, "Mutual Insurance Company,"
http://www.investopedia.com/terms/m/mutualcompany.asp

[2] Carlos Lara, "The Policy Loan Debate Explained," *Lara-Murphy Report*, September 2014

[3] Lara, "The Policy Loan Debate Explained"

[4] Lara, "The Policy Loan Debate Explained"

[5] Lara, "The Policy Loan Debate Explained"

[6] Investopedia, The History of the FDIC,
http://www.investopedia.com/articles/economics/09/fdic-history.asp

www.ingramcontent.com/pod-product-compliance
Lightning Source LLC
Chambersburg PA
CBHW050737180526
45159CB00003B/1264